FORTUNATE SON

FORTUNATE SON

My Life, My Music

JOHN FOGERTY

WITH JIMMY McDONOUGH

LITTLE, BROWN AND COMPANY

New York • Boston • London

Little, Brown and Company
Hachette Book Group
1290 Avenue of the Americas, New York, NY 10104
littlebrown.com

First Edition: October 2015

Little, Brown and Company is a division of Hachette Book Group, Inc. The Little, Brown name and logo are trademarks of Hachette Book Group, Inc.

The publisher is not responsible for websites (or their content) that are not owned by the publisher.

The Hachette Speakers Bureau provides a wide range of authors for speaking events. To find out more, go to hachettespeakersbureau.com or call (866) 376-6591.

Unless otherwise noted, all photographs are courtesy of John and Julie Fogerty.

ISBN 978-0-316-24457-2 (hc) / 978-0-316-38773-6 (large print) / 978-0-316-35189-8 (signed B&N edition) / 978-0-316-35369-4 (signed edition)
LCCN 2015943212

10 9 8 7 6 5 4 3 2 1

RRD-C

Printed in the United States of America

For Julie...
I love you more than the sky

CONTENTS

CONTENTS

FORTUNATE SON

INTRODUCTION

Beautiful Dreamer

IT ALL BEGAN with a record. A children's record.

My mother, Lucile, was a teacher at a nursery school about half a mile from our home, down a dirt road. I remember walking there a few times when I was four or five years old. By myself. That's how innocent our town—El Cerrito, California—was then.

One day, at around this time, my mom brought me home after school and gave me this record. It was a small-size children's record, and nearly the first object I would have realized was my possession—mine alone.* My mom sort of made a presentation of it, and we listened to it together.

The sound of it! Like a bolt into my brain. On each side of this record there was, of course, a song. For all I know the artist could've been Fred Merkle and the Boneheads, but I sure do remember the songs: "Oh! Susanna" and "Camptown Races."

---

* Actually, my *very* first possession was a doll. A black baby boy doll. I carried that thing around with me everywhere until I was three or four years old. I've often wondered if that somehow predisposed me to love black music, black culture.

3

And for some odd reason my mother explained that Stephen Foster wrote both of them. He was a *songwriter*. That's just a fascinating direction for my mom to go in. When you're explaining "Rudolph the Red-Nosed Reindeer" to a child, you don't tell the kid that the songwriter was Johnny Marks. But my mom sat me down and explained this to me. A lot of things have happened in my life, but this one made a huge impression. And like I say, I wasn't even four years old.

"Camptown Races" I thought was an odd title, because it sounded like "Doo Dah, Doo Dah." But there was a certain flavor to the song that I liked. "Oh! Susanna" was even better! I liked how they sounded. They seemed *right*. I don't know another way to say it, yet I have that feeling to this day—I feel the rightness of a song when it's tight and works, from the words and music to the heart. I considered them amongst my favorite songs. So Stephen Foster became very important to me.

Just a mom, a kid, and a little record. I am still kind of dumbfounded and mystified by this. I have actually wondered if my mom had some kind of a plan—if she knew the gravity that this moment would have for me, each day deep into my life. The simple act of my mom saying to me, "These songs were written by Stephen Foster," set a tone. Opened a door.

When something hits you that hard, even when you're three years old, you begin to watch for it, to crave it. And every time I heard about Stephen Foster, I took note of the song. "Old Folks at Home" (a.k.a. "Swanee River"). "Old Black Joe." "My Old Kentucky Home." "Beautiful Dreamer." There were a lot of them. Over two hundred, I'd learn later.

The stories, the pictures, the way the songs were told—I really took all that to heart. Foster's songs seemed historic, part of America. It was important—in the same way that Mark Twain became important to me. This stuff all felt like the bedrock of America, like the *Mayflower,* or the way that we grow corn in

Indiana. These were things that I didn't realize as a kid—whatever it was, I just knew I really, really liked it.

So when it was time for me to evolve and be my own artist, there was Stephen Foster. Riverboats and the Mississippi...I mean, "Proud Mary" could've been written by Stephen! And then there was that moment when I realized that when I did that sort of thing, it was *good*. It resonated so strongly when I got it right— not always immediately and sometimes even decades after a song's first inspiration hit me. I began to encourage myself to go deeper in that direction.

Now, if you had told me when I was fifteen and playing for drunks in some dive like the Monkey Inn that I was gonna some-how combine rock and roll with Stephen Foster, I would've told you that you were crazy.

People would listen to my songs and ask, "Where does this come from?" I had trouble explaining that. I hadn't been to Mis-sissippi when I wrote "Proud Mary," nor had I been to Louisiana when I wrote "Born on the Bayou." Somehow it all just seemed familiar to me. Still does.

In recent years, I was fascinated to learn that even though he wrote all these songs about the South, Stephen Foster was from Pittsburgh! I think he wrote "Swanee River" long before he'd ever been to the South. There were other parallels between our lives. Stephen was tricked out of his royalties. And there were parallels that could have been. Foster ended up alcoholic and dying in pov-erty at the age of thirty-seven. A pretty sad but typical tale. And if it hadn't been for my wife, Julie, that would've been me.

I didn't get into music to get girls. Or to become famous. Or rich. Those things never even occurred to me. I got into music because of *music*. I just loved it. It was (and is) a mystical, magical thing. I just wanted to write songs, good songs, *great* songs, ones that

JOHN FOGERTY

Stephen Foster might not cringe at. "Proud Mary," "Born on the Bayou," "Have You Ever Seen the Rain," "Lodi," "Who'll Stop the Rain," "Green River," "Fortunate Son"—chances are you might know a few of those.

Now, if you're familiar with that last song you might be surprised to see it as the title of my autobiography—*Fortunate Son* has even been used for the title of a biography of George W. Bush!* So how do those two words apply to me? The best way I can illustrate that is by sharing a story about something that happened recently—on Veterans Day.

I was performing on a broadcast called *A Salute to the Troops: In Performance at the White House*. It was hosted by President Obama and the First Lady and shot on the south lawn of the White House, and shortly after being shown on public TV it was broadcast around the world via the American Forces Network.

Being part of this special evening was a big honor for me. The producer of this event was Ken Ehrlich, who also produces the Grammys. Years ago, Ken and I had teamed up for another event in Washington to honor Vietnam veterans. This time, Ken and I and Julie felt that "Fortunate Son" was exactly the right song for the occasion.

Among other things, you could call it an anti-war song, and there was some pushback over my choice—"No, we don't want him to do *that* song." I was very respectful: if the powers that be were too scared and didn't want me to do it, I wasn't going to make a stink, because I was there to play for our veterans, a group of guys and gals I sure have respect for and feel somewhat akin to. It's been a long relationship, you might say.

So everyone was a bit on eggshells—President Obama was sit-

---

* Apparently George W. is a fan of my song "Centerfield"—I've been told it's on his iPod. Which always makes me wonder: has he heard any of my *other* songs? Like... "Fortunate Son"?

ting right up in front, and I'm sure he was wondering, "Have I made the right decision to let this go forward?" When I went to the mic, I said, "I just want to say what a great country we live in, and God bless the men and women who protect us." With that, my band and I tore into the song. I ripped into the guitar riff and all the troops stood up. Here I was, standing there and shouting out the lyric, "It ain't me! It ain't me!," and all these veterans were like frat boys, yelling out the words and just having a great old time. There was a four-star general among them. Even the president was bopping away. It was the coolest thing.

I finished the song to a huge reaction. Returning to the mic, I said, "And I *am* fortunate." I had thought about this—I wasn't sure I was going to do it until the very last moment—but I said those four words and I left the stage. Meaning, "Yeah, that's my song. Yes, I believe every word of it. But look who I am, look at what's happened for me. My dream came true." I was also saying, "What a great country. We do this in America, the land of the free. They don't do this in North Korea." In that way I truly am a Fortunate Son.

We had another introduction all ready to go for this book. It was pretty action-packed, with all the bells and whistles. A lot of razz-amatazz. Cinematic, even. It had Robert Johnson, Bob Dylan, roaring guitars, and a cast of thousands. I think Richard Nixon might've even had a cameo. But you know what? It wasn't me. I'm not a flashy guy. I'm pretty simple and from the heart. And that's how this book should be. Miss Julie pointed all this out.

Julie. You'll see that name a lot in this book. I'm not joking when I say I'd been waiting my whole life to meet her. If you're a friend of mine, you understand that she's the love of my life. You'll be hearing from Julie directly later on. She knows everything there is to know about me. It's powerful to have someone you can be so open with, and by the time you reach this book's last words, you'll know as well as she does that I'm not afraid of the truth.

Julie's a big reason I'm doing this book. She's quite aware of the emotional content in things. In the old days, I tended to not talk about it. I can yak for three days on the subject of James Burton's guitar playing. Meanwhile, something that involves anger or fear or trepidation or uncertainty I wouldn't say two sentences about. In the old days, if I was talking about some conflict or controversy regarding my band, I'd downplay it. I didn't want to sound like a whiner and I really didn't want to throw mud all over Creedence — that was still *my band*.

So I'd end up talking about things in a surface, almost scientific way, not revealing my true feelings. I'd circle around but never get to the heart of the matter. This is my chance to finally set the record straight.

I'm not going to sugarcoat things or make excuses for anybody, especially myself. Hell, I'm not running for president. So I don't have to hide anything. It's very freeing to make up your mind and let it all hang out. Once you shine the spotlight on your own failings, there's little else that can touch you.

I'm just going to tell you my life story the way I see it.

This is the story of a kid from El Cerrito and his musical dream. It came true, and then it turned into a nightmare. His record company betrayed him and so did his band. Worst of all, he was pulled away from his music, from the songs that to this day mean everything.

Stick around, though, because, unlike so many stories about the music business, there's an honest-to-God happy ending.

CHAPTER 1

El Cerrito Days

I WAS DRIVING HOME the other day with my wife, Julie, and our daughter, Kelsy, after a long day out and about. It felt right— all of us warm and comfortable together, content from our day. Suddenly I had a flash of a memory, something that I hadn't thought about in a long time. It reminded me why I cherish these ordinary moments with my family.

My mind was back in a time when I was in the ninth or tenth grade, and I needed to get the homework for that day, which I'd somehow missed at St. Mary's High School. I'd been instructed to pick it up at the house of my friend Michael Still. He answered the door with his younger brother, both of them in nice robes and pajamas, looking freshly scrubbed. My friend apologized for their pj's, saying, "My mom likes us to get our nightly bath over with before dinner so we can relax." *Relax.*

I remember standing there, feeling all that warmth and happiness flowing from their home, thinking about how these boys were really taken care of. Even though I was just a kid, the disparity between my friend's life and mine was pretty clear to me: he was going to stay home and relax, and I was heading home to a cold, empty house and my drab cement basement bedroom that often flooded. There were no dinner plans—my mom was working, and my dad no longer lived with us. And no, I wasn't going to relax.

I was born on May 28, 1945. I grew up in El Cerrito, California. Years ago I made the mistake of filling out some questionnaire that asked where I was born, and since there's no hospital in El Cerrito, the correct answer is Berkeley, which is what I answered. But I didn't live there and I wish I'd reasoned that out, because now when my childhood is mentioned, it's always attributed to a place that's not my hometown.

I am proudly from El Cerrito. And warm predinner baths and robes or not, I dearly loved my early days and wouldn't trade them with anybody. El Cerrito certainly stamped a different view on me than what some hustling street kid in New York City would have gotten, or a songwriter growing up in Nashville. They're more savvy about stuff. Basically nothing came from El Cerrito, although the baseball players Pumpsie Green and Ernie Broglio both attended El Cerrito High School. I do feel really lucky to have grown up in a little town.

Things were unhurried. Everything was close and friendly and familiar, not nearly so fearful as things can seem these days. There was a little row of businesses near my house, with Bert's Barber Shop, the Louis grocery store, a drugstore, a beauty salon, and Ortman's Ice Cream—you could get a slush for a quarter. When I had a paper route, that was a daily thing.

Man, I'm not even that old but I lived in a different time. I grew up before rapid transit. A six-year-old kid could walk around by himself, head over to the market with a nickel in his pocket, and buy an apple. I remember going over to talk to the butcher to get bones for my dog. You could walk to school. I'm sure the class sizes were actually fairly large, but I recall them being intimate. The teacher looked right at me and talked to me. I had some teachers I really liked. My second-grade teacher, Mrs. Fuentes. Miss Begovich, my sixth-grade teacher. She talked about education and intellectual things in a way that mattered. Miss Begovich was inspiring and always gave me a lot of time.

Officer Ray Morris was the local police officer. He rode a three-wheel motorcycle—a memorable thing, for sure. But the reason I know his name is because he was, in a sense, my commanding officer. I was in traffic patrol in fifth and sixth grade—a lieutenant with a whistle and a sweater. And Officer Ray Morris was in charge.

Once I sent away for a siren that you could attach to the front wheel of your bike. I added an old stove timer to that, so when I pulled up to a place, it would go *roooooooowrrrrr DING!* Outasight. One day I'm blazing down Fairmont Avenue, going all of twenty miles an hour, and I blast right through the Ashbury Avenue intersection by the school, revving my siren and timer. And Ray Morris is sitting right there on his three-wheel motorcycle, just shaking his head. He didn't come over and yell at me—the look was enough. He'd show up at our Boy Scouts meetings too. Once, my bike got stolen and it was no time before he got it back. When I look back now, it's remarkable how close and interwoven all that stuff was in my life. It was community.

Children—I prefer their world even now. I'll bet I have every episode of *SpongeBob SquarePants* committed to memory. Same with *Hannah Montana* and the Wiggles' TV show. I sit and watch the shows with my kids. A child can sit and think about one little thing for eons. Adults can seem short and snippy to them. They don't dive into things. They're in a hurry. Kids are aware of that other, grown-up place, and they think, *It's okay—if I don't do anything too bad, they'll leave me alone.*

So you wander around in your own little world, mostly unfettered by what the grown-ups do. I know I did. At the drugstore near my house, there was a soda fountain. I'd put my ten cents on the counter, they'd take some syrup and fizz water and make you a soda fountain drink. There was a little moment one time when I was sitting there, staring at the Green River soda label on the syrup bottle. It's an old-timey illustration of a yellow moon over a river between two banks—now it reminds me a bit of the Sun Records logo. It really struck me, like, "Wow, I'd like to go there." Green River—I saved that title in my brain, filed it away. Why did I care about that? I was eight. But I was absorbing everything, everything I thought might be important for later in my life, even if I didn't know why. That's what you do as a kid. Everything matters.

El Cerrito had a drive-in movie theater. We always called it the "Motor Movies." When we lived at 226 Ramona Avenue I had the room over the garage and the top bunk of a set of bunk beds. I could watch the movies from my bed. I remember watching *Gentlemen Prefer Blondes* and, I believe, *Moulin Rouge* through my bedroom window. And various monster movies that my mom wouldn't let me go see!

Us kids would ride bikes on the grounds of the drive-in, and I regularly climbed up inside the screen to the top. Next to the drive-in was an old adobe building called the Adobe Restaurant. My mom told me that the place used to have slot machines, and I learned it may have been a "house of ill repute" in the '30s and '40s. Strangely, when they closed the drive-in and a shopping mall was about to be built, an arsonist destroyed the Adobe (perhaps clearing the way for that property to be included in the new mall). I remember going through the ruins and finding square metal nails from the early 1800s.

There was a really cool place to play that was not too far away from our house. It was called Indian Rock and it was just a big bunch of boulders. There were a couple of passageways you could squeeze through. A great place to play hide-and-seek.

Of course, the ultimate play place had been the high school itself when I lived across the street on Eureka Avenue. It's a wonder any of us kids survived. I remember all these big pipes that were one and a half to two and a half feet in diameter. We were little, so we could crawl inside those things and shimmy down to the other end and hide. Kind of like in the movie *Them!* Jeez! It would have been so easy to have gotten sealed up inside there. No one would've found us...ever. Then there were the piles of sand and gravel—I guess they made concrete out of that. And ropes hanging everywhere that you could climb up and slide down. I think the jig was up when we found a whole bunch of glass. It was probably meant to be windows for the classrooms, but for us aspiring baseball players it made a perfect target! Busted...

One sunny morning me and Mickey Cadoo had a day for the ages. I was about four years old. First we had climbed some small apricot trees and stuffed our pockets with green (unripe) apricots. Then, after eating a few of these, we decided to "climb to the top of the high school." They were still framing the building up on the top floor, and there was a lot of exposed wood crisscrossing and not nailed down. Somehow we managed to get all the way to the top level and stand up on the frame. There was nothing but sky above us.

I had seen cartoons where guys slip on a banana peel, so to make it even more dangerous, I untied my shoelaces, letting them dangle. There was a long, thin board that was just lying across the two sides of the framed space, maybe ten feet from one side to the other. The board was about six inches wide and perhaps one inch thick. So as I stepped out onto this board, it began to bounce up and down. Right about this time, I noticed my dad down in the front yard of our house, which was just across the street. There I was, fifty feet in the air, calling down to my dad, "Hey, Dad, Dad—look at me! I'm up here!"

Well, my dad looked up and saw me there, and his heart must

have stopped. I remember that he started jumping up and down, almost like dancing, arms waving in the air. And after a few shocked exclamations, he began to say, "Don't move, Johnny! Stay there, stay there. *Do not move!*" Somehow I stayed put and my dad clambered up the structure and got us to safety. Whew.

I lived in the El Cerrito area until I was forty. In 1986, long after I'd graduated out of traffic patrol, El Cerrito declared July 15 John Fogerty Day. That little ceremony was very small and sweet, the mayor spoke, and a few fans came from far and wide. Usually when somebody gets these things it's because they invented something or cured a disease. In my case, the official proclamation mentioned songs: "Whereas Mr. Fogerty has written 'Proud Mary' and 'Down on the Corner'..." Not everybody has a day set aside by their hometown, so being honored in that way is pretty untouchable to me. Whatever happens for the rest of my life, I will always remember that fondly.

I loved the song "Shoo-Fly Pie and Apple Pan Dowdy," and when I was a kid I sang it everywhere. Apparently, one Sunday morning at church I became filled with the spirit and broke into the song. I started dancing, and to illustrate the lyric I made my eyes bug out while I rubbed my naked tummy. The folks in church got a big kick out of this bouncy, diaper-wearing baby belting out "Shoo-Fly Pie." The more my parents tried to shush me, the more my "audience" laughed. I'm told I created quite a scene. Two years old and already on the road to perdition!*

I can remember riding in the car in the dark back then. Nighttime. And my parents were singing to each other. With no accom-

---

* My parents converted to Catholicism when I was two. They had me baptized, and yes, I remember it. I did *not* like it. Somebody held me while the priest poured water on my forehead. I thought, *You trying to drown me?!*

paniment. They would sing a lot of old American and Irish standards, like "By the Light of the Silvery Moon," "Shine On, Harvest Moon," "Little Sir Echo," "Danny Boy"—things like that. They weren't singing to the radio, they were just singing with each other. They'd do one song they called "Cadillac"—"Cadillac, you got the cutest little Cadillac." I asked my parents about that one. I thought it was odd that somebody would write a song about a car. They explained to me that it was actually a song called "Baby Face," and they had changed the words. When Little Richard's second album came out, he had both "By the Light of the Silvery Moon" and "Baby Face" on there for the parents, and this made total sense to me.

Listening to my folks sing was really nice. I realized even then that it sounded full. I'd sit between them and sometimes sing along. If one of my parents sang a different note that complemented the melody of a song that I knew, like "Jingle Bells," I'd get curious—"That sounds good, but what are you doing?" They told me they were *harmonizing*. My parents were very good at it.

So that's where I first heard about harmony: sitting in the front seat in that old car with my parents. A little later, in public school, probably about the fourth grade, Mrs. Gustavson would come in and teach music for an hour once a week or so. That's where I first learned "The Erie Canal Song" and "This Land Is Your Land." There was some American songbook we were learning from. Sometimes there would be a piano accompanying us, and sometimes we were just doing this a cappella. And I always looked forward to it.

Everyone was singing in unison, all singing melody, and I'd sit there and start singing harmony. I really had fun finding a note either over or under what the class was singing. And because there were forty kids singing *their* part and only me singing *my* part, it felt pretty safe to experiment. I was drowned out a bit, but I could hear it. If it was wrong, I could quickly change before anybody heard. Both my regular teacher and my music teacher would take note that I was somehow harmonizing—and knew what sounded right. Without being told. One day we were singing "Come Now and See My Farm for It Is Beautiful," and Mrs. Gustavson looked over as I was singing away, and I said, "Is that okay?" She said yes and smiled.

Sound was one thing and lyrics another, and I have cared about both practically forever. My dad and I were in the car once, talking about the song "Big Rock Candy Mountain." We liked that song and he was explaining it to me. It seemed like a really fun place. Then we got to that "little streams of alcohol" part. I asked my dad, "What does that mean? What's 'alcohol'?" He said, "It's something grown-ups like to drink. That would be fun—a whole river full of it, like if there was a whole river of soda pop!" It's ironic: here I was, asking a guy the meaning of "alcohol" when I would eventually learn that he consumed far too much of it. And so would I.

There's certainly a lot of musical influence from both of my parents, but probably more so my mom because I was around her a lot more. My mom played what was called stride piano: her left hand would play a bass note and then a chord, and the right hand would be doing melody and also some syncopation. It was cool, kind of like boogie-woogie. And she was appropriately sloppy. It sounded kind of barrelhouse.

My mom would play the piano and sing "Shine On, Harvest Moon," and sometimes I'd sing along. This was after my parents split up. When you're a kid who's a little rambunctious and rebellious, sometimes you join in, sometimes you act like it's corny and not cool at all. But "Shine On, Harvest Moon" is still one of my favorite songs. One of the best versions is Oliver Hardy singing it in a Laurel and Hardy movie, *The Flying Deuces*. That version of "Shine On, Harvest Moon" was truly inspiring to me. Laurel is dancing, doing a kind of soft shoe, and Hardy is singing. It's a thirties musical arrangement, but Oliver is more bluesy. And he sings really good! Even though it was slapstick for the rest of the movie, this was serious. Nobody laughed at this. At least that's how I took it: they were presenting art.

There were five boys in our house. We were pretty rough-and-tumble, it's a wonder we didn't all end up in San Quentin. It would've been so easy to fall in with the wrong kids. None of us had any trouble that way, really. My parents—especially my mom—kept my brothers and me on a fairly wholesome path. Whenever I got too close to the edge, my mom would pull me back. I'd call us lower middle class.

My mom was a social person, kind of gregarious. After my parents divorced, she got a teaching degree and dealt mostly with emotionally and even mentally challenged young people. She knew an awful lot about that stuff—I say "that stuff" because us boys really didn't know a lot about my mom's work. Her job was across the bay in South San Francisco, so she left pretty early in the morning and didn't get back until almost dinnertime. That's a lot of day we had to ourselves, and we turned out all right.

I don't know how my parents met. They came to California, to the Bay Area, from Great Falls, Montana. Lucile—my mother—was born there. That's a cool place to be from, Montana. I can remember my parents talking about the mosquitoes being so big they could open the screen door and let themselves in. Around 1959—either before or after I was in the ninth grade—my dad took my brothers Dan and Bob and me on a trip to Montana. We had stopped at a railroad crossing, and my dad pointed and said, "John, look at that train. Trains are really beautiful. And they're going away." I think he said it was a steam engine. He got the message across—that this was important and it was too bad the steam train was going away, and more so an era. My dad had quite an affection for trains. I have a feeling he spent some time riding the rails. The folklore in our family is that my dad hoboed all the way to California.

My father, Galen Robert Fogerty, came from South Dakota and grew up on either a ranch or a farm. My dad was Irish. The way I heard the story is, either my dad's dad or his grandfather had escaped the potato famine in Ireland by moving to England. Our family name used to be "Fogarty," but there was a lot of prejudice against Irish people in England, so to disguise that fact, they changed the spelling to "Fogerty." To my mind, that's kind of like changing the spelling of "Smith" to "Smythe."

England proved unsuitable too, so they came to America. I grew up feeling very strongly about being Irish—leprechauns, the pot of gold, the Irish whiskey—and I took note that the Irish are pretty good at sitting around a pub and putting down a pint.

My mom's roots go all the way back to the *Mayflower*. Her distant relative was William Gooch—he was English, and the first governor of Virginia. George Washington was born in Goochland County. I liked the fact that we had roots going way back in our country. Family legend has it that we were related to Daniel Boone. Another story I'd heard was Davy Crockett.

My dad worked at the *Berkeley Gazette*. Speaking of appreciating trains and beautiful things going away, he was a Linotype operator, setting type for the paper each day. Then he took a second printing job, so he was not only working an eight-hour-a-day job, he was working after that. In other circles, other times, he would've been called a man of letters. Well-read. Even though I believe that my dad graduated from college back in Montana, in our lifetime, it never really translated into a better job, into making more money or offering any change to our station in life.

That may sound selfish, but I don't mean it that way.

My dad was a dreamer.

He wrote stories. My dad had a movie camera in the forties, for taking movies of our family. I still have some of that film (and even use it as a backdrop in my show). And he would sit and edit different pieces of it on this editing contraption that he had. But he also had some stories that were filmed about a character named Charlie the Chimp. My dad wrote a story about the discovery of Pluto. I think it might've appeared in *Reader's Digest*. I believe that was the biggest thing he ever got published. In later years, my dad really identified with Ernest Hemingway: he had the white beard, white hair. There were a few manuscripts lying around the house. I think my dad really had the goods as a writer, but he was never able to get it across. There are many people in this world like that: they're artistic and yet they don't know how to meet the right emissary, that person who's going to publish their work and get it out there. Dad wasn't able to pull off being a famous writer. Or even one who gets paid for his work.

He was always on the fringes, smart and in the moment. He had invented a little game that I had when I was three or four. It was an educational toy: little round cardboard disks, each disk had a letter and a number, and every disk was a different color. There were shapes, colors, letters, and numbers—that's how I learned my alphabet, how to count, and the names of colors. It was a cool idea! Looking back on it, why couldn't he have made a million dollars with that? He never hooked up with the right people, I guess—maybe never even tried—so we just had it in our house.

Like I said, Dad was a dreamer. I tried to write a song about it I don't know how many times. The way I felt about it even as a fourteen-year-old kid was, "Dad isn't practical. He doesn't bring that dream into the real world. He doesn't do something about it." Being a dreamer, I know that can be a good thing. But when it came to my own life, the idea was, "Don't be just a dreamer. *Do* something." The lot of the dreamer is, he gets to hold bricks made out of mud. He never finds the gold mine. It's always some turkey like Rupert Murdoch. Or Saul Zaentz, for that matter. For me, I wanted to do both. I wanted to dream and I was going to try to be more successful.

Now, my dad was successful in so many other ways, like exposing us kids to nature. He loved camping and the outdoors. I didn't really learn to fish from him, but I think I wanted to know how to fish *because* of my dad. He also read stories to us when we were really little, stuff that was cool and informative to his family of five boys. "The Shooting of Dan McGrew" and "The Cremation of Sam McGee" by Robert Service were favorites. Tales of the Yukon and gold-mining camps. One of the greatest scenes in "Sam McGee" never left me, the part about this guy who was really cold and died. He froze to death. Well, firewood was scarce, so they threw him into the incinerator, right? Then a little later in the story they open the door to throw in some more logs and the guy they threw in there goes, "Hey, would you put another log on the fire? It's getting cold in here!" That was just cool to me.

Sometimes we'd visit Davis or Dixon or other small towns up in the central valley of California. I remember being in Dixon for the Fourth of July one year. There were fireworks and jungle gyms, swings, a lot of green grass....Further up Interstate 80 were the Giant Orange Stand (which was shaped like a big orange) and the Milk Farm Restaurant. It was a really warm, happy, cozy feeling. My parents liked to go to places like that. And they transferred that love to me. I really have a love of interesting little American towns—it's an idyllic way of life, at least to an outsider. Almost like a Norman Rockwell painting.

Some of my happiest memories are of Putah Creek. It was a wild creek up near Winters, in Northern California—"going to Winters," my family called it, and every summer we went. In my childhood we went to Putah Creek five or six years running. Putah was a picturesque, slow-moving little creek. We stayed in a small cabin. I remember that cabin fondly—it had a wooden, green screen door. I don't know why that's important to me. We rented it from a guy named Cody who was around seventy-five years old, tall, very thin, wore a hat. I was told that he was a direct descendant of Buffalo Bill Cody.

Not far from the cabin was a rope that hung down from a tree, over a little shallow spot in the creek that was ours when we were there. There's home movies showing my brothers swinging out and dropping in the water. My dad helped us kids make slingshots out of Y-shaped twigs with elastic bands cut from an old car tire's inner tube. We didn't hear talk about, "Well, you can put some-body's eyes out" or "Don't break those windows over there." There was so much open, free space. It was woods and brush, hardly a car anywhere—you really had to go far to see any peo-ple. All day long we could wander around. Once I even found an old, decrepit abandoned house.

The air was fresh up there, but when I breathe deep and think back, it isn't of grass and sky. My dad had a canister attached to a pump that he'd use to spray for mosquitoes. It had a certain sort of smell, kind of like paint thinner. I remember that smell fondly. It brings it all back.

I learned how to swim in Winters—when my older brothers, Jim and Tom, dared me to stick my head underwater. One day I learned how to float on my back. I was up early and the rest of the family was asleep. I floated across to the other side of the creek. I think it got deep enough in the middle that I couldn't stand up. When my dad came out of the cabin and saw me on the other side he just freaked out. I was a little afraid he might whack me.

Once in a while my dad would go with us into the actual town of Winters. There was a little grocery owned by this one family that owned the liquor store and the gas station too. My dad would give me a dime or a nickel to get a soda, usually a Nehi Orange. Or cream soda. Or lemon-lime.

Boy, I looked forward to Putah Creek. One time, when my brother Bob was a baby, there was some discussion about going to

Los Angeles instead. My dad said, "We'll have the baby decide." He wrote down "Winters" on one little piece of paper and "Los Angeles" on another piece. They put baby Bobby down and let him go. For a while he was crawling toward the "L.A." I remember I didn't want that. Finally Bobby went over to the "Winters" piece of paper and we all went "Yay!," so happy that we were going back to Winters.

After we stopped going, I'd think back fondly about our trips, even as a kid. I was possessive about Winters and Putah Creek. In my memory, they were *mine*. My vacation place, my special little spot. I always felt really good there. Number one reason, I think, is because my parents were relaxed there, as they used to be when they'd be singing songs together.

Things change and sometimes they change a lot and leave just bits of what mattered behind. Sometimes the best things stay around only in our heads. At one point back in those days, Dad drove us in the car high up on a hill, and we were looking down at the little town of Monticello, and he said, "One day that will all be underwater." I had no idea what that could mean. How could that be? Are people going to walk around underwater?

I think Dad was saying good-bye to our idyllic Putah Creek. In fact, they did dam up the creek. Now it's called Lake Berryessa, a big man-made lake. I drove my motorcycle up there in the seventies and I think I found the spot where the cabin would've been. It was all overgrown, just bushes, remnants of wood. I couldn't find the actual cabin. I think even then it had long since fallen down.

CHAPTER 2

The D Word

FOR FIRST GRADE, my mom enrolled me in a Catholic school in Berkeley, the School of the Madeleine—or the School of the Mad, as us kids called it. It was a few miles away—which doesn't sound too far, but all I know is it took a half hour or more in the morning and many's the time I ran out of the house to catch the bus and missed it.

Our teacher was a twenty-year-old named Sister Damien, who was in her first year. She was just a kid. And throughout that year she had several unhappy episodes. Sister Damien was overwhelmed. In the end we heard that she had a nervous breakdown. One time she was mad at the class and kept us all after the bell. "You can't leave. You have to stay in your seats and not a peep out of you." And this little second grader comes in, he's got his rag, and he dutifully starts polishing up the platform that Her Majesty's desk is sitting on. He's busy and doesn't turn around to see the whole class sitting there. Suddenly Sister Damien just slaps him across the face—*wham!* That was indicative of the atmosphere.

To get to school, I would leave my home alone and walk two blocks to catch the 67 Colusa Avenue bus across from the Sunset

View Cemetery in El Cerrito. Then I'd ride all the way to the top of Solano Ave, in Albany, and get a transfer from the bus driver. From there I would catch the F train, which went into Berkeley and passed behind the School of the Madeleine. The conductor would let us off behind the school. Mind you, I'm in the first grade doing this—six years old! Every morning at eight o'clock the students would assemble in the playground and then march into class to the music of John Philip Sousa. If I missed the 7:05 bus, I was going to be late to school, which happened many times. There was a chain-link fence surrounding the playground, and they locked the gate at 8 a.m., so I would have to climb the fence and run to class.

By this time I've been away from my home for maybe an hour. And at around nine thirty or so, something would happen. And it would happen over and over again, okay?

I'd raise my hand and say, "Sister, I have to go to the bathroom."

"Not now," she'd say.

After that, she just ignored me. Again, this isn't, like, one time. It was enough times that it was a normal occurrence.

I'm sitting there in my uniform, blue shirt / salt-and-pepper corduroy trousers, taking my pencil and poking the cracks and crannies in my desk. Oh, I'm squirming. I'm like Alan Shepard in the space capsule. "Houston?" "Yes, Alan." "I gotta go wee-wee. Is it okay?" "Uh, wait. We'll get back to you." You're holding it, you're holding it, and then you can't anymore. Finally, you give up all rules of social convention. It's too late.

And then you're hoping nobody will notice. But Kenny Donaldson noticed. "Sister Damien! John Fogerty has a puddle under his desk." And even then she wouldn't call on me. So I had to sit there until there was a break, and then I had to clean it up. And sit in my moist clothing for the rest of the day. This happened probably two dozen times over the course of the school year. I'd get detention after detention for wetting my pants—I guess they figured if they punished me enough, I'd stop having to pee.

So one day at lunchtime I found myself looking at the water fountain. It had a white porcelain trough and three faucets. Now, fresh in my mind is getting detention, because I drank water and then had to pee. Under the trough, I see the knob to turn off the water and I'm thinking, *Oh, I can help everybody here.* I turned off that fountain. *Wham!* When they found out I was the dude responsible? Another detention and a note home to my parents. At the end of the year, the rest of the class was being rewarded with a trip to the circus. Not Johnny Fogerty. Because I was such an uncontrollable little wild man, I had to stay home. I was a bad boy.

The next year, my mom put me in Harding Grammar, a public school two blocks from my house. I could walk to school! And things were normal. I thrived. I really loved it there.

Okay, so how many of you have had the "flying dream"? For me this was a common occurrence as a kid. In the movie *E.T.: The Extra-Terrestrial* there is a scene where a bunch of kids are following E.T. Suddenly, they are all up in the air (flying!) and then they "fly across the moon." That scene made me cry and I still don't know why.

There was a period from about the third grade to about the sixth or seventh grade where I had this flying dream a lot. It was almost always the same. Every night, I would fly around my little town, just above the trees and telephone wires, looking down at the houses and people. I was accompanied by a "friend" who seemed to be acting as a guide. As far as I can remember, we always saw the same stuff. Looking back at this from many years later, I find there is just enough room in my head to believe that perhaps this was an E.T. encounter. *O-o-o-o-EEEE-o-o-o.*

One day in sixth grade Miss Begovich noticed an odor in our classroom. "What is that smell?" she said. Most of the kids didn't seem to notice it and couldn't identify what it was or where it was coming from. Suddenly, this kid Fred blurts out, "John Fogerty smells." Of course, now everyone is looking at me, and I start to go into confused mode. *Like...huh?* But Fred is adamant—"Yes, it's John, he *smells!*"

So Miss Begovich gently says, "Well, John, maybe you should go to the bathroom and figure this out," or words to that effect. I stand up and start to head to the washroom, not really understanding what I should do. Suddenly, Kathy, a girl I'd known since preschool days, stands up and says, "It's me! *I'm* the one who smells!" Now my emotions are completely topsy-turvy.

Kathy insists to the teacher that she is the one who should go to the washroom, and of course this whole scene is being played out in front of the entire class. My head is spinning. *Whoa...this girl is taking a bullet for me.* I'm filled with emotions that are hard to describe. I realize that she is a very brave person, a very *good* person, to do something like this. It is such an honor to have somebody do that!

Finally, Miss Begovich decides that we should both go to the washroom, thereby defusing some of the guilt, I suppose. I went to the washroom not really knowing what to do, so I peed, washed my hands, and headed back to class. In the hall, I ran into Kathy and I thanked her. This is one of those times in life where I wish I could go back to that person and really express how amazing that made me feel.

After school a few days later, a couple of us kids were working on an extra school project. This one kid, Yvonne, had been absent for more than a week with an illness, so Miss Begovich asked us to clean out her desk so we could send some books and schoolwork home to her. Among the books and papers, we found a dead bird—in her desk. *Y-e-e-o-o-w!* We were kinda grossed-out. Miss Begovich said, "That was probably the bad smell from the other day." The next day she quietly explained it to the whole class...

*   *   *

So much of the flip side—the good side—of those years was rooted in music. I was born with the gift of curiosity, and if I heard music I liked, I just had to find out all about it. I got into the blues at seven. It was really because of doo-wop. There was no rock and roll yet!

My two older brothers were listening to rhythm and blues, and KWBR in Oakland was mostly doo-wop and R & B, meaning black music.* They played records like "Gee" by the Crows and "Ling, Ting, Tong" by the Five Keys—we'd try to decipher the crazy Chinese references. It all seemed so exotic. Later, it was "Death of an Angel" by Donald Woods and the Vel-Aires—he's talking about his girlfriend dying, but it was so cool! Kids love death! (Much later I found out that the Catholic Church *banned* "Death of an Angel" because their position was that angels can't die. Even cooler!) Thirty years later, when Ozzy and all those guys were shouting at the devil? Same kind of deal: it was something forbidden, behind a veil and unspeakable, and therefore music that parents don't like. A lot of the music I was hearing was pre-rock and roll, but it had so much of the vibe.

Intermingled there on KWBR was some real blues—urban blues, even some country blues. I remember hearing Muddy Waters in the early fifties, and then Howlin' Wolf came along with that *voice.* I loved that voice—"Wow, listen to that guy. And the name!" I'd listen mostly by myself. Bouncin' Bill Doubleday was the deejay from three until six, and then Big Don Barksdale had a show at night. On Sunday they played gospel. That's where I first

---

* One of the major sponsors on KWBR was a product called Dixie Peach Pomade. I imagine that in those days it was used by young black guys to straighten their "do." I rode on a bus all the way to Swan's Drug Store in Oakland to get this stuff. It was great on a "flattop" or on longer Elvis hair. Plus, it smelled good!

heard the Staple Singers, "Uncloudy Day." The sound of that guitar—God, what a cool thing. That vibrato: *bewoowowow*. Even as a kid I could identify that sound right away. Pops Staples was doing all that. I loved that sound. The Swan Silvertones might've been my favorites. It was spiritual, church stuff, but I was mostly interested in the music.

By the time I was eight years old, I was using my mouth (and my body) to imitate the R & B records I was hearing. Every day I'd walk a couple of blocks from my house down to Harding School. There was that time to be alone, that precious time. I spent a lot of it thinking about music. I'd make the sounds of the band that I was hearing in my head. I'd go along and imitate Ernie Freeman's "Lost Dreams" or Bo Diddley's "I'm a Man"—*daaaaah daaaaah da dummmm*. Sometimes I'd snap and clap and all that, but mostly I just did it with my mouth. Or my throat. Or hummed it. Grunts and hums and noises. Sort of...guttural sounds. Probably sounded like I was coughing to the outside world, but I loved making the sound of the bass and the kick drum. Nobody I knew of was doing anything like this, but I was quite comfortable with it. That was my way of making music.

It would hypnotize me, walking to school doing that. I even had a little friend who walked with me sometimes who called me Foghorn Fogerty—that's what he thought I sounded like when I made my noises. I still do that, actually. I hear music in my head and I make those guttural sounds to catch the vibe.

I even invented a persona, a group called Johnny Corvette and the Corvettes. It must've been right around 1953, because the Corvette had just been introduced and every kid loves sleek, sexy lines and a big, fast motor to die for. Everyone in my mind's band had matching jackets, like the Turbans or the Five Satins or the Penguins. I was Johnny, and we were black. I meant no disrespect— I was just a kid fantasizing about what he loved. So in my mind, the grown-up version of me and my group was black.

* * *

The first house we lived in was right across the street from El Cerrito High School, at 7251 Eureka Avenue. That house stayed cool in the summer. I have good memories from there.

But we moved about 1951, and I turned six in the new house, at 226 Ramona Avenue. I remember that time being less happy. My parents split up in that house.

I think working two jobs got to my dad. I remember my mom actually saying a couple of times that he was working way too hard. I think my dad went kind of crazy.

He had a nervous breakdown and was up in Sonoma or Napa, where we went to visit him, and I'd think, after seeing him, that we were all getting back together.

I didn't see most of the fighting personally, but as I understand it, my parents had a long, messy split. One night we all went to the drive-in to see a Bob Hope movie called *The Lemon Drop Kid*. When we came home, I went to sleep. My brothers Tom and Jim were awake and our mom and dad were fighting over something. I only heard about it the next day.

Apparently my dad was pointing his finger angrily at my mom and she bit his finger. And there was blood all over the place. Luckily, I didn't see that particular fight either. I can tell you I never went to see *The Lemon Drop Kid* again. When it comes on TV, I'm still, like, *click!* "Sorry, I ain't watchin' that." There was something in that movie that caused bad stuff to happen.

The whole idea that my parents had separated and then divorced was upsetting and very traumatic for me. It really cut like a knife. It was something I couldn't actually even talk about. The *D* word. And nobody else was talking then either—there were no divorce jokes on sitcoms. Though I'm sure divorces were everywhere, I didn't know any other kids whose parents had divorced.

At school, if there was some kind of paper I had to fill out answering "Who do you live with?," where I had to state that I lived with my mom—*only* my mom—I was mortified. Because that initiated the inevitable questions: "Where's your father? Has he joined the...foreign legion?" That's a phrase I heard more than once. It was a shameful thing, having only one parent. I took it really hard. Almost like it was my fault.

When my mom and dad finally divorced is hazy. When I was near the end of the third or fourth grade—I can't quite remember—we were all going to move to, I think, Santa Rosa. I was about eight. So I informed all my pals that I'd been with pretty much since kindergarten that we were moving. But I know I didn't seem to be that upset about it—the way you see kids being torn apart from their roots. I just remember that I kind of explained it to everybody. Then come next fall when school started, there I was, back again! And there were all my friends that I'd already said so long to.

"John, what happened?"

"Well, my dad moved."

I remember just feeling unworthy and kind of like, "I gotta slink home and never talk about personal things." I didn't quite know how to approach the subject, because I don't think I really understood.

The main issue for both of my parents was the fact that they were both alcoholics. Believe it or not, I had a real aversion to alcohol as a young person. Seeing my parents in a drunken state and hearing them talk in an incoherent way? It was repulsive to me.

I really used to kind of rag on my mom. I was a typical kid, dissatisfied with my parents. There was one meal we hated, liver and onions, because the liver would never be cooked. All us boys would just be repulsed. My mom would kind of be in her cups, acting funny—and we didn't know why, because we never really saw her drink. I think she hid it in a cupboard or something. That was part of our lifestyle more than I care to admit, and far more than any kid should ever know about. I used to say I got negative examples from my mother. What *not* to do.

I'm a lot more forgiving now, especially with my mom. And that's not just because I realize the good she instilled in me from when I was real young. It's because, man, human beings are fragile. We break easily if things go wrong, especially if you feel hopeless. Oh God, that's the worst thing for any of us. Frustration is a very powerful and almost insurmountable thing. I'm sure my mom had a lot of heartbreak. She had five boys that were quickly turning into five men that she had to deal with and try to raise right. On her own. I think my mom tried valiantly. God knows she tried.

So I want to do right by my mom. I worry about disclosing so much—always have. In the world I grew up in, you didn't reveal things that you considered nobody's business. Now that she's gone, I'm really just trying to tell the story, to get to the truth of her experience and mine.

In many ways my mom was remarkable. She educated me on many subjects, exposed me to a lot of music, and showed up for things in my life. I'm very grateful for all that.

And I see the whole situation a little differently now—not nearly so much from the point of view of what I was missing, what I didn't get. Because these days I have so much, because of Julie. I see both of my parents almost as tragic figures. It's a shame that for so much of her life my mom probably felt unloved, that she wasn't taken care of. My dad certainly never found love after the two of them split. That was all a waste. The real tragedy? Before all the economic struggles and alcohol started ruining everything, I think my parents actually loved each other.

We had a record at home called "When You Were Sweet Sixteen" by the Mills Brothers, an old 78. My dad and mom used to sing that together. God, what a song. Beautiful. It breaks my heart to hear it now. I was just a kid watching his parents divorce and this was their song!

* * *

I remember us boys stuck in some courtroom. All five of us, without our parents, being called into a room where an official person, I assume a judge, asked each one of us directly: which parent do you want to stay with?

I think we had all agreed we wanted to stay with our mom. I don't know if we had gotten our stories synchronized, but I know that in our hearts we all felt like that was the best solution. But it was really scary that this even would happen, being asked this question by a grown-up, a stranger.

It was difficult to have to think about that. Mainly I just wanted to stay with my brothers. We wanted to stay together.

My parents were continually arguing over all the manifestations of divorce. There was one Saturday morning when us boys had been camping overnight in the backyard in our sleeping bags, when suddenly the police arrived. Here we were, just kids in our own backyard, being awakened by the police. Apparently we were supposed to be with my dad that Saturday and Sunday.

My dad was being pushy by sending the cops. And he was supposed to pay alimony, but he wasn't doing it. I don't know if he had a job or not. And my mom was basically withholding us. I'm sure my mom was within her rights. She would make comments like, "Well, y'know, I could have him put in jail, but what good does that do anything?" It wasn't going to change our situation.

All I know is, I was being woken up at eight o'clock on a Saturday morning by the police saying, "You have to go with your father." Maybe I didn't even want to go with my father.

I didn't see my dad much after that. One period it was one weekend a month. We'd go to a movie. Those kinds of things are just so awkward, at least in our case. It kind of petered out to where I really didn't see my dad at all. For years.

*   *   *

A few years later, when I was in the eighth grade, my civics class—which was all the kids I knew in junior high and a lot from before that—went on a field trip to Richmond, the county seat. They drove us down in private vehicles—a couple of station wagons, not a big school bus. And we went to the courtroom.

We all file in and sit down, maybe twenty of us. There's a case going on. A divorce case, ironically enough. I heard one teacher tell another afterwards, "Y'know, I'm not really sure that was something the children should've seen."

Both parties were there, the husband and the wife, and it's the wife who's wanting to leave the husband, not the other way around. The wife testifies a little bit, and she's fairly matter-of-fact. I don't want to say cold—just straightforward.

Then we watch this poor man talking about his family, his wife. And he's being grilled by the wife's attorney. This moron lawyer is pointing an accusatory finger at him. He's like a bulldog and he is just *killin'* this guy. We're watching, dumbfounded. It's like television, but it sure ain't *Father Knows Best,* y'know? Finally the husband, who is now very emotional, says, "Well, perhaps my wife would consider a reconciliation. Maybe we could get back together." He's made himself so vulnerable in front of everybody. Like a little boy. That was unexpected. I'm a twelve-year-old kid who had never imagined such a thing before. I don't know anything at all outside my parents' divorce. At that point I didn't even have a serious girlfriend yet. I'm thinking, *That's real sad.* I was shocked and hurt and everything else. It's hard to revisit this, even now.

But their case is done for the day. Because the husband can't go on. I see the attorney look over at the woman and she's got her arms folded. She's a tough one. And the husband's broken down, just blubbering. So the judge goes *boom, boom,* with the gavel. "We'll adjourn until two weeks from now."

We're all just sitting there, and the clerk comes up to read the next case—this is God's honest truth. He says, "This is the case of Galen Robert versus Edith Lucile Fogerty. Can we hear the case? Are either of the participants present?" Well, that's my mom and dad, of course. It had been four or five years and they hadn't finalized the divorce.

They say the name Fogerty twice, and the judge asks, "Are any of the parties here?" And somebody says, "No, your honor, they're not here." And the judge says, "Okay, we'll continue this at a later date."

But the damage has been done. I thought, *How in the world did that spaceship ever land on me? I gotta be in court and hear that? With my classmates?*

So we get back in our vehicles for the trip home and I remember that Sandy, one of the girls, said to me, "The Fogertys they named in court—is that your parents?"

And I said no, tryin' to act cool. I got real...stiff. Not myself. They had *no idea* that it was my family. I pulled it off...or maybe I didn't.

The kids were all jumping up and down in the back of the station wagon and I was acting kind of weird. Not like a kid. Obviously I was in shock. The others thought I was kind of snooty because I wasn't laughing. And somebody made the comment, "Oh, yeah—he's too mature for us." Kids can be so unaware of how much, and how little, they know.

My dad stayed angry 'til the end. Late in his life he lost a leg to diabetes. He was in and out of the hospital, and we were over there to move him out of his apartment. All the brothers got together to help.

There was his old television, from way back in the day, in a metal case made to look like wood grain. And the metal had all these big dents in it, and in some places even perforations. I recognized that from before. When I was a kid my dad would get so pissed trying to make the picture come in he'd give the TV a few whacks.

Back then we had taken a trip to Montana and had rented a trailer and hitched it to the back of our '56 Buick. A little trailer with a kitchen and a couple of beds. There was a little compartment over each wheel with a door that hung down and locked. This was where they stored a hose for filling the water tank in the trailer and other small essentials. We noticed that the door had several dings on it, almost like it had been hit with a sharp instrument. Well, a week or two later we were deep into our trip, perhaps in the middle of Yellowstone National Park. The car was overheating, so my dad would have to use the hose to siphon water from the trailer into the radiator. He parked the car and we all went back to help. The door was open and the hose was gone. We were screwed! Apparently, the latch on the door was faulty and wouldn't stay closed. My dad got really angry and started hitting the door with a hatchet. Then it dawned on us kids: those marks we had noticed on the door were the same marks my dad was now making with the hatchet. Apparently, the last poor guy with this trailer had gone through the exact same thing.

Now Dad started to kick the trailer. There were a couple of expletives coming out of his mouth. He may have even had the hatchet in his hand. There's my dad, just kicking the crap out of this trailer. Most of the time my dad was very thoughtful and peaceful and calm. I was kind of shocked—a kid watching his dad lose it. This was a whole nother guy—a guy that, truth be told, was a lot like me. I've had a temper since I was very young. I can remember another kid coming up to me during kickball and saying, "You know, you're gonna have to learn how to control your temper." It was noticed by my teachers in grammar school too.

So years later, when we were moving my dad, there's that old banged-up TV. This was some time after Creedence had broken up, and it wasn't like I was livin' on Happy Street. But I looked at that TV and realized that my dad was seventy and he was still that way. I thought to myself, *I don't want to get old and die being so ornery, so angry.**

Being a teenager has to be the toughest time for almost everyone. Especially if there's anything you perceive as wrong in your world. I felt put-upon, unworthy. Behind the eight ball. Divorce was an immense failure to me. Huge. It just didn't happen to good families.

There was an overall aloofness that I would have. The fact that our economics really went downhill after the divorce certainly made it worse. I felt that I was at the bottom end of the social totem pole. I sure wasn't as bad off as some guy living in a shack in Mississippi with no plumbing and no electricity. But somehow I felt poor. Between that and my parents' divorce it was almost too much to bear.

After I'd been at St. Mary's for ninth grade and half of tenth, one of the teachers said to my mom, "John seems so sad, reserved. He's just really quiet. Is there something wrong? Is Johnny okay?" And my mom would try to say, "Oh, no—he's just thoughtful." Even I would say it. Most all of the pictures of me as a kid show that thoughtful, pensive side. I'd always have my eyebrows knot-

---

* Happily, my mom was able to find love after all this turmoil. She met a wonderful guy named Charles Loosli, and they got married on June 11, 1977. I got to spend time with Charles and Mom in later years. We all loved Charles.

ted together. Sadness may not be quite the right word, but if that's not the one I don't know what is.

I was ashamed of the house we lived in. The furnace never really worked right—it was run-down. This was a middle-class suburban neighborhood, but we had the worst house on the block. Around the seventh or eighth grade, I moved into that concrete basement that flooded every winter. There would be an inch and a half of water on my floor, and I got to laying two-by-fours so I could get from outside my room to my bed without stepping in the water.

I had a clock radio. My first radio had been one of those art deco plastic ones—a funky color, bluish gray, a Philips or an Emerson. Then, with my paper route money, I upgraded and got a clock radio that plugged in and was supposedly going to get me up—it had an alarm. At some point the knobs came off. I liked to take things apart, so I was probably to blame, but now it had no knobs—just metal posts. One morning I was standing in the water and decided to turn on the radio. When I grabbed the metal posts, I got quite a jolt. I'm lucky it didn't kill me.

I liked to listen to the radio before school, so when the alarm went off, dang it if I didn't figure out how to propel myself forward from the bed, stand on the little wooden sill on my closet to avoid the cement and water, turn off the alarm, and fall back to bed listening to the music. Every morning that was my little dance. Directly above my bed there was a metal grate for the furnace, so when my mom was leaving for work in the morning, she'd stomp on that grate and go, "Oh, John! Oh, John! Wake up!" *Thump, thump, thump.*

You know that Brian Wilson song "In My Room"? It's the *truth*. Your room is your sanctuary. That basement room was my place to be me—"I'm not hiding, but I'm *in my room.*" Upstairs with the family was a bit chaotic, challenging, whereas in my room I had Duane Eddy, Elvis Presley, Bill Haley, the Coasters. They were in the windows—literally. We didn't have window shades for the basement, and if people in the next house were in their garage, they could see right into my room, so I put my record albums up to cover the windows.

Music was my friend. I absolutely loved to listen to it. I surrounded myself with it, thought about it all day. I think my interest only intensified after my parents split. There was joy in music. And for some reason, I don't know how or why, that joy only confirmed what I'd known since I was small: that it was for me.

CHAPTER 3

My Influences

BY THE TIME I got to the fifth grade, I thought, *I need to be able to earn some money.* I think my mom was giving me a quarter for an allowance. At that rate, I was never going to get anywhere.

The *Oakland Tribune* had to be delivered at 4 a.m. on Sunday, but you needed an adult to take you around in a car, and my mom wasn't going to do that. So I got a paper route at the *Berkeley Gazette,* the small paper where my dad had worked, and they didn't deliver on Sundays. The place to pick up the papers was only two blocks from my house, right by the cemetery up at the top of Fairmont Avenue, and my route was just down all the streets across from Harding Grammar School.

My route was only about thirty-five papers. If things were okay, I'd make twenty, twenty-five dollars a month. But it turned out that some people were unscrupulous. I had thirty-five customers, but sometimes I'd get stuck with forty newspapers. Those were called extras, yet you were financially responsible for them. You had to get on it, call the *Berkeley Gazette* and say, "You're givin' me five extra papers. I don't have forty customers—I only have thirty-five." I think they did this sort of routinely, because it kept happening to me. This went on for months. They'd stop, and then they'd start again.

Finally I'd had enough. I turned the tables on them. I'd receive thirty-one papers for thirty-five people. Then I'd go right to the front of the Louis store, where they'd have the papers for sale in a little stand. Customers would take a paper, drop their ten cents in the box. Honor system. Well, I'd go over there and take the four I needed and go off and deliver them. I did this until I got my money back, not a cent more.

I was really mad. But my paper route money allowed me to buy things, and the things I liked to buy were records.

Forty-fives were the coin of the realm. If there was a hit song you liked, you bought the single. The very first time I ever bought 45s, it was the Platters' "The Great Pretender" and "At My Front Door" by the El Dorados. They were Christmas presents for my brothers Jim and Tom. Tom and I shared music even pre–rock and roll. There was a song called "Billy's Blues" by Billy Stewart. Tom really liked that song. This was before the Internet days, and man, you could not find that record anywhere. So I went to my mom-and-pop record store at the mall, Louis Gordon, and even though it was a year and a half late, I got them to order that record, and I gave it to Tom for his birthday. I knew it was precious, better than a million dollars, because you just couldn't get it.

I can hear and see the little record player I'd bought with paper route money as if it were yesterday. It was red and white and had three speeds. That was a boon to guitar players, because you could slow down 45s to 33 and try to learn the solos. The record player had a funky speaker. Certain records, like "Susie Q" by Dale Hawkins, really skipped, so you'd have to put a quarter or a battery on top of the tonearm. I liked to put the first Elvis album on when I took a shower.

I first saw Elvis on the Dorsey Brothers' TV show in January 1956. He had that whole juvenile delinquent thing that kids love. I was a kid, so I was drawn to the danger of it. I don't think I was playing guitar yet. After the first or second time I saw him, I was standing there in front of a mirror with a broom, practicing the sneer. I was hypnotized without even realizing why.

It was the other side of "I Want You, I Need You, I Love You" that really grabbed me. I was up visiting my dad, and we were in some little grocery store with a jukebox when I heard "My Baby Left Me." I went, "*What* is *that?*" I ran over there to see. "It's Elvis!" "My Baby Left Me" is one of the greatest rock and roll records ever made. That guitar was just...so...great. Man, it had attitude and attack. It was a big part of what made the record special. Scotty Moore *invented* rock and roll guitar. Even though I didn't know his name and I wasn't a musician yet, I just knew right then: "Whatever *that* is, that's what I wanna do."

I tried to buy the first Elvis album while I was at my dad's house in Santa Rosa. I had four dollars and fourteen cents. I walked all the way to the mall and they were sold out. I ended up buying Bill Haley's album *Rock Around the Clock*. The guitar playing on the song "Rock Around the Clock" was way ahead of everybody else. It was kind of jazzy—Danny Cedrone was older, more advanced than your average rock and roll guy. It's only been in the last dozen or so years that I can play that solo!

A week later, I got that Elvis album. That and the Bill Haley album I knew backwards and forwards.

I saw Elvis at the Oakland Coliseum in 1970, when he was just speeding through the songs—the whole Vegas thing with the karate moves. Elvis had recorded "Proud Mary," which, of course, was a tribute and an honor, but it seemed like he hurried through it. I guess if I were more tactful I wouldn't say that. Yes, it was great to have your idol do your song, but you just wished that he had killed it. I never got to meet Elvis, and I really wish I had. Elvis got crazy, but he just lost his way. And we have all done that, whether a little or a lot.

I took Elvis very personally. Even as a kid, standing there at the record store, paper route money in hand, I was really thinking about value. I thought about buying an Elvis 45, but Elvis was in the "Big Hunk O' Love" / "Doncha' Think It's Time" phase. And I was already thinking, *Yeah, but Elvis isn't really rock and roll now.* This was in 1959, still the beginning of Elvis's career! In my mind I had noticed a kind of softness, a pop ethic in Elvis, and if I'm going to a desert island, I better have rock and roll. So this time I bought "Red River Rock" by Johnny and the Hurricanes instead.

Still, Elvis was Elvis, and in the fifties you had Elvis and you had Pat Boone. Elvis was obviously cool, but Pat Boone just... wasn't. Now, don't get me wrong: Pat Boone made records that I actually like. "Bernadine." "Love Letters in the Sand." "Moody River" was outstanding. Then there are the really sappy ones, like "April Love." I used to hear that song in my head at the oddest moments. Much later in life, I'd be hunting up in Oregon, climbing up a long, long ridge uphill, I'm sweating, out of breath, and I'd take that first step onto the flat ground on top, and suddenly there it would be in my head: *dumdumdum DUM...* "Aaaaaa*april love!*" I'd go, "Where did *that* come from?!" Like it had been waiting to happen—my own personal soundtrack.

Pat seemed like a really decent fellow, but he was almost *too* nice. And so was his music. I sure didn't want to be sappy, but I didn't want to be a bad guy either. In those days, it was, "Do you wiggle like Elvis or do you croon like Pat? Which gang are you with?" I struggled with that. Well, not really.

Through Elvis I discovered more Sun records. "Ooby Dooby" by Roy Orbison and "Blue Suede Shoes" by Carl Perkins. As an eleven-year-old, I had the same exact connection with Carl Perkins that the Beatles did. There were times when I actually thought Carl was way higher up than Elvis, because Carl could play *and* sing *and* write songs. That combination made a big impression on me. In baseball, Willie Mays was what they called a five-tool player. To me, Carl was the musical equivalent.

Go back to the "Boppin' the Blues" / "All Mama's Children" and "Blue Suede Shoes" / "Honey Don't" singles, and listen to that twangy thing in Carl's voice. His singing is killer! Those two singles are still, like…perfection. I bought "Blue Suede Shoes" three or four times because I was wearing them out! I'm still astonished at how great "Blue Suede Shoes" sounds. There's so much air. And the groove of the band, that country boogie thing—whew. Just untouchable.

I met Carl in Memphis on my 1986 tour. It was like meeting God. He said the nicest thing. Chips Moman, the producer, was with him, and Carl said to Chips, "The way this guy writes, imagine what Sam would've done with him if he'd walked into Sun." Here's somebody I idolized, *Carl Perkins,* giving *me* some cred? Talking about Sam Phillips and Sun Records and me? What a dream. I just ate that up.

Years later I was doing a fund-raiser for Bill Clinton, and out of the blue, Carl showed up. He mentioned that he was making a record with Tom Petty. I wasn't going to let this opportunity go by. I just looked at him, my face a question mark, and I said, "*Well…?*" And he looked at me and said, "Well, John, I'd love it if you'd come and do 'All Mama's Children' with me." Carl knew that was my favorite.

Our version is not as good as his original—how could it be? But I'm glad I got to do it. Especially because of this memory: While we were recording, I came back from the powder room to find Carl sitting there with a Stratocaster, and he was just rippin', playing this really mean, nasty stuff. Just vicious guitar. I was taken aback. He was sixty-four, he'd already had some surgery and a heart attack, and I was thinking of him as older, vaguely fragile. And here he was, just slayin' it, in tone, vibrato, and attitude. For a moment I could not believe it.

Then my mind did this little double take: *Well* of course *Carl can play like that*—*he's one of the two or three guys who started it all. He was right there. Why should I be surprised that he sounds that way?*

Carl passed in 1998. And to this day, I still have his number in my phone.

I've mentioned hearing the blues at age eight. As I was growing up listening to KWBR, it was a flood: Muddy Waters, Howlin' Wolf, B.B. King, Elmore James, John Lee Hooker. Wolf had a gigantic influence on my singing—"Big wheel keep on *toinin'*." But I didn't realize it at the time. It just seemed natural to me.

Fast-forward to August 1968, and Howlin' Wolf is opening for Creedence, which mystifies me even now. I stood in the audience and watched Wolf's whole set. He was a big guy, and he'd point that finger at you. I think he was sitting down most of the time, but this was not some old guy going, "Blah, blah, blah"—this was life and death. Hubert Sumlin was on guitar, a 335 Gibson, and he was badass. He had a youthful look, like Floyd Patterson when he won the heavyweight championship. We got to go in the dressing room, and I felt like a little kid. The Wolf smoked Kools and so did I at the time. We shared a smoke. I'm sure he was amused. He looked at me like he was going to reach down and pat me on the head.

There's a handful of guys you keep coming back to, and for me, a lot of them are the kinds of guys who can't be copied. Why has no one *ever* done Jimmy Reed since Jimmy Reed? *No one* has been able to do it. Jimmy had a bunch of harp solos that were really high. Jimmy played up there where nobody else went. And he's not in a hurry on the guitar. There's a couple of funny notes here and there. That's his signature, those notes. Because he does them all the time! I listened to "Honest I Do" about three times the other day. Man, it's just such a feel. Everything is for a reason and a purpose. That band is *locked*.

I saw him only once, at the Berkeley Community Theatre in 1964. Jimmy was drunk. *Drunk.* His guitar was out of tune, and he was sitting down. I remember after three songs that were kind of incoherent, someone in the audience yelled, "Tune up!" In those days, we were all prim and proper—to do that to an icon, it had to have been pretty bad. I was so sorry to have seen that. Later you find out he'd gotten screwed out of his record royalties so he's pretty bitter, and he's an alcoholic. Oh, really? Even though later I went through the same stuff, I think seeing all this as a young guy was informative, in that it made me not want to end up there. I was no better—don't get me wrong. It's just that I saw tragedy in it.

The music that was new when I was a kid was *hot*. I bought Bo Diddley's first album. In my eyes, Bo was like Elvis. That was the first fight I had with the guys in my band. We got paid, like, twelve dollars total for a gig, and instead of buying new strings, I took my four bucks and twelve cents and bought Bo Diddley's album. "*What?!* Why did you do *that?!*" "Because there are several songs on there I think the band should learn, like 'Before You Accuse Me.'" Much later we recorded that one. I rest my case.

That first Bo album was just chock-full of stuff. "Who Do You Love?," with its human-skull chimney and cobra snake for a neck-tie....I was fascinated by the imagery. Many times I've said there's a part of my writing, my imagery, that's kind of spooky and weird and about dark places. Well, I walked into that room through Bo Diddley's door. The song "Bo Diddley" is probably my favorite. Spooky as all get-out. That whole child-rhyme thing—if that ain't the most primitive mumbo jumbo! Yet it sounded so full on the radio. I don't even know if there is bass on that record. It doesn't matter. Then you have Bo doing his thing on guitar, especially the solo. It's just hypnotic. Bo magically fell into a thing that was just so hot because of the deep drums. The tom-toms, the maracas—it's really tribal. Even now, that drum is so big—*bum da bum da bum*. A lot of bands have come down through the years trying to do the Bo Diddley beat and haven't come close.

Man, I was *lucky:* I saw Ray Charles live several times right around the "What'd I Say" time. He had that old beige 120 Wurlitzer (later I got one myself). He played saxophone—that was amazing. The big album for me was *Ray Charles in Person.* Has a better live album ever been made? It was recorded with one microphone in the audience by a deejay from a local Atlanta station. It was an outdoor summer show, and because of the acoustics of the space you can almost hear the hot air. God, the sound of the instruments. Obviously they didn't have echo machines. It's live. It's natural. "The Night Time Is the Right Time"—Ray's version is way more soulful than Creedence's, which is more rock and roll, screamin' guitar. That live album has "Drown in My Own Tears." Everything is just so slow. He's wrenching every last ounce of feeling out of that song. That album had a huge effect on me, and its influence still lingers.

Little Richard is another one whose influence on me is total, complete. We played together at the Grammys in 2008 and I finally got to tell him, "Richard, man, I've loved you since I was a little boy." He's probably the greatest voice ever in rock and roll. I really mean that. His performances on those classic rock and roll records are perfect. "Lucille," "Keep a Knockin'," "Good Golly, Miss Molly," "Send Me Some Lovin'." They are like textbooks of how a rock and roll singer should sound. A couple more that have always meant so much to me—"Long Tall Sally" and "Slippin' and Slidin'." Like they say, "It don't get any better than that!"

Even as a kid I loved dissecting a recording. The music behind it all was just as important to me as the vocal. I thought Gene Vincent was *great*. His records were like instrumentals to me. "Lotta Lovin'," "Woman Love," and of course "Be-Bop-a-Lula." I'd sit and play him on my record player, and in my mind I'd block out the vocal. Because there was all this *great stuff* going on back there. *Man!* That was an education to me: *Without the singing, it's like an instrumental.* And as you'll soon see, that's how I presented the songs and the arrangements to my guys in Creedence. Gloriously, I grew up in an age when there were instrumental rock and roll records with lots of guitar. They were very important to me as a kid, and a great way to learn.

Like "Honky Tonk" by Bill Doggett, from 1956. That's an incredible record. It was big-time important to me as a kid. Side one of the single is the guitar side, side two the sax. Both are incredible. It's just that groove. As a kid, I decided one night that I was going to learn "Honky Tonk." I put the record on and practiced. By the way, I played it in F, like the record. That's hard, because it means you're fretting every single note. In recent years I've checked out some of these online forums, and lo and behold, there are guitar nuts talking about playing "Honky Tonk." Comments like, "If you're gonna play that song, be a man and play it in F!" If you play it in E, it's a lot easier. The Ventures did that and turned it into more of a rock and roll song.

"Hide Away" was another song that just killed me! A Top 40 record, it wasn't just on the R & B station. Freddie King was a huge influence on my guitar playing and my musical knowledge in general. He's playing a shuffle, but the piano player is kind of straight, and the drum is somewhere in between. It's the coolest feel, especially in this age of computer music, where everything's locked together in a really boring fashion. My first band, the Blue Velvets, played almost as many Freddie King songs as we did Duane Eddy. One of the songs we always played was "Just Pickin'."

This might surprise people, but "Flying Home" by the Benny Goodman Sextet is one of my favorite records. It's got a great feel and I just loved that melody. My mom talked about Benny Goodman, so as a kid I just went ahead and got my own copy of the 1938 Carnegie Hall concert. I don't know much about the other big band guys, but I figured out everything I could about Benny Goodman. Once I discovered Charlie Christian's guitar on that record, I became interested in him and wound up buying and collecting everything of his that I could find. I've listened to hundreds of hours of Charlie Christian.

I'd say there's a whole lot of Charlie Christian in how I play. Just the feel of that swing, the way he riffs off the melody. Parts of "Keep On Chooglin'" are referencing Charlie. In my head, when I go Americana, and I hear that soft shoe happening, like "Shortnin' Bread" or "Down by the Riverside," and I'm trying to keep things just real simple, I'm probably in some way referencing Charlie Christian. Not that I'm as good as Charlie!

Speaking of that feeling you have when you make music that clicks, when I was a kid there was a lot about the record *Rumble* that was absolutely right. The guy's name was *Link*. Link Wray. Oh my God. That record was really important. The song sounds like the title: "Rumble"! *Blang blang blang.* It's so...menacing. When that was a hit on the radio, all kids were tuned in to it—not just me. Everybody understood: *Man, that's so cool.*

Some guys rightfully become known as guitar gods, and Duane Eddy was a huge influence. James Burton was behind Ricky Nelson, Scotty Moore was behind Elvis—that was usually the way. But Duane was his own front man. The name on the record was his. "Rebel Rouser" *killed* me. Real melody, that honky sax, and those guys back there modulating every twelve bars—what made him *do* that? It's just cinematic.

"Three-30-Blues"—as a guitar player, "Three-30-Blues" was a high moment. I used to practice that with my band, and I still play that song. Some people might say, "Oh, that's a simple blues." But it's a *mighty* simple blues. I heard Duane play that at the Oakland

Auditorium with B.B. King on the bill. Fantastic. I heard later that B.B. sidled up to Duane and said, "I sure like that 'Three-30-Blues.' " Only Duane Eddy sounds like that. He means every note.

I learned so much from his early albums. The thing I noticed was that all of his songs had these great titles, like "Forty Miles of Bad Road." Cool song, but I realized he could've called it anything—it didn't matter, because there's no words. Duane came up with these descriptive titles that created a mood to match the feel of the music: "Rebel Rouser," "Cannonball," "The Lonely One," "First Love, First Tears." This was instructive to me as a songwriter. I was learning what went into a good song, and Duane helped me see that having a great title was a big part of it.

I think influences can come from anywhere. The sound of a bee's drone or a truck's Doppler effect as it drives further down the road. And of course the TV. I became aware of Ricky Nelson through *The Adventures of Ozzie and Harriet.* I was already watching the show like the rest of the world. Rick was doing the cool things that teenagers did, like washing his jeans in the shower. They sprung his recording career on us in an episode where Rick plays football—which Ozzie likes—and plays music, which is what Rick likes. Rick did "I'm Walkin'," and the next week he did "A Teenager's Romance," singing with his eyes almost closed, eyelashes fluttering. He was sixteen years old and impossibly good-looking—no flaws! By "Stood Up," the fourth single, Ricky had shanghaied a young guitarist named James Burton from some country band. When I heard James going *dangadangadanga,* oh man, I knew something had changed. This was rock and roll ground zero. I was totally on board! When I saw them do the song on TV, this cool dude was playing guitar behind Ricky. During traffic patrol in sixth grade, a girl asked me if I liked music, and I said, "I like that guitar player with Ricky

Nelson. He's really cool." I didn't even know his name. I didn't even play guitar yet!

The main music coming out of Rick Nelson was rockabilly, as opposed to Frankie Avalon or Fabian or Bobby Rydell, or even Elvis by then. I was lucky enough to get to posthumously induct Rick Nelson into the Rock and Roll Hall of Fame in 1987. Sam Phillips was sitting right down there in the audience. I looked at him and said, "Sam, he gave you a run for your money." Ricky Nelson was doing rockabilly—pretty urgent, even dangerous, stuff. Even when he did "Lonesome Town," he just killed it. That was a slow ballad, but it wasn't sappy and dumb: it was rock and roll guys playing a ballad.

I remember listening to his version of "My Babe" over and over and over. That guitar was like, "Oh, *yeah!*" In some ways that record was better than Little Walter's original. It was *James.* James just shines and sparkles, and Ricky clearly knew this, because there was always a James moment on those singles. Listen to "Believe What You Say." There's the greatest guitar solo you ever heard. Basically, the world stopped. Ricky was letting everybody know there was this wild genius in town. Scotty Moore, James Burton, and a few others in the world at that time were inventing cool rock and roll guitar. And James was all of eighteen!

I thought Ricky seemed like a very normal teenager. A nice guy. I liked that a lot. Elvis was spending his money recklessly, buying big rings and Cadillacs—I worried. I just thought that was really extravagant. Ricky was just a kid living at home. He seemed like a good role model. I never heard about temper tantrums, anything scandalous—he struck me as mild mannered, not showy, not crazy. I know that sounds boring, but to me that was an admirable trait. I'll go to my grave saying this, although lots of folks would disagree: you don't have to be crazy or a lunatic to make good rock and roll. I know guys who make really great music and they're solid dudes and family oriented. They value that sort of thing. Like Bruce Springsteen and Dave Grohl.

Rick wanted me to produce him back during my long, dark time. It was 1978 or '79. I was in no shape to handle that. I couldn't even produce myself, let alone one of my heroes. At least I got to meet him. The very last time I saw him was in Memphis, recording a tribute to Sun Records in the eighties. He was singing along on one of my songs, "Big Train (from Memphis)."

An interesting bit of musical history (at least to my mind) is connected to that solo in "Believe What You Say." One of my favorite records of all time is a song called "Party Doll" by Buddy Knox and the Rhythm Orchids from 1957. Starting with this song, I became a very big fan of Buddy and the sound he was making. The drum part on this record became very influential, as it was maybe the first rock and roll song to feature a "two-one" back-beat. I was fortunate enough to meet Buddy Knox in the late eighties, and I mentioned the drum part to him. He was proudly aware of the milestone and immediately responded, "Yes, but it's reversed" (which it is).

Anyway, Buddy had another big hit that year called "Hula Love," which I also had as a boy. Then he seemed to disappear. To a kid, a few weeks is an eternity. Anyway, time passed, and suddenly here was another Buddy Knox song called "I Think I'm Gonna Kill Myself." I *loved* that record, but you couldn't get it. I had to order it at my little record shop and wait for weeks. Apparently, the subject matter of the song had gotten it banned in some places.

So now to the point: "I Think I'm Gonna Kill Myself" featured a guitar solo that sounded exactly like the solo in "Believe What You Say," and I was certain of that for years and years. After hearing it recently, I can now see that they are not the same. They are, however, in the same key and played in the same very high register. Back in the late fifties, the Telecaster was just about the only guitar you could reach those notes on. I thought about the mystique of these two solos many times over the years, so when I met Buddy Knox I asked him about it. His answer was "I don't know if they're the same, but it sure was some great playin' by Cliff Gallup." Man, was I excited by that answer. Only us guitar geeks care, I suppose, but Cliff was the guy on "Be-Bop-a-Lula." And *he* disappeared too! (By choice.)*

In the summer of '57 I was working up at the Russian River in Healdsburg, California, and "That'll Be the Day" was all over the radio. They had a big outdoor PA blasting that song. I just went crazy. Rockin' guitar, rockin' drums, harmony singing, the lead guy's voice—I just knew them as the Crickets then. And that riff! It all sounded so damn right.

Every artist had a band, but the focus was usually on the singer: Elvis, Ricky. With the Crickets, it was presented as the Crickets. It was *the band*. This was just a different approach, and their debut album, *The "Chirping" Crickets*, had that picture. Four guys in suits, all four holding the two guitars, but they're looking straight into the sun! There's Buddy trying to smile, but the sun is shining right in their faces, so they're all squinting. You can tell these were not rich guys. They ran up on the rooftop of a big building in New York City to take that shot. It's a fairly unflattering picture. That picture told a story, though. One that the Beatles would only refine. The wisdom of keeping it a singular image, not being ragtag—like, for instance, the Grateful Dead. Being a little more showbiz about it.

I had made up my mind that Buddy Holly was one of those people that I was going to follow for his entire career, buy every

---

* The Rhythm Orchids had quite a year in 1957—"Party Doll" and "Hula Love," both million sellers by Buddy Knox, and another million seller, Jimmy Bowen's "I'm Stickin' with You," *plus* Jimmy's "Warm Up to Me, Baby." I bought all four of them.

record he made. I had already gotten the first album and a few singles. I still had a paper route in the eighth grade, and getting the papers one day I saw the headline that Buddy Holly, the Big Bopper, and Ritchie Valens had died in a plane crash. So years later, when Don McLean's "American Pie" came out and he talks about delivering papers with the news "the day the music died"? I thought, *Wow, I actually did that.* That was a sad day for rock and roll.

I got ahold of a Buddy album in 1965 or so, on some off label, and there were unreleased versions of songs, one of which was "That'll Be the Day" in the wrong key. It's nothing like the version that became the big hit, and I was quite sure Buddy was rollin' over in his grave. Maybe collectors enjoy all that, but as an artist, I cringe at the idea. The artist goes through a process of evolution to get to the recording that he wants to present to the public, and the rest is not presentable. It was meant to stay behind closed doors. I knew I didn't want that to happen to me, so I would always destroy my outtakes—for instance, an earlier unrealized version of "Mystic Highway," or the first version of "Wrote a Song for Everyone." They can't put it out later if it doesn't exist!

There were a few records from the rock and roll era that seemed to be in another place from everything else. I obsessed over these:

"Deep Feeling" by Chuck Berry
"Lost Dreams" by Ernie Freeman
"Honky Tonk" by Bill Doggett
"Blue Moon" by Elvis Presley
"For Your Precious Love" by Jerry Butler and the Impressions
"Little Boy Blue" by Bobby "Blue" Bland
and more recently:
"Island Style" by John Cruz

I think I first heard country music on television. I was four years old. There was a show called *The Hoffman Hayride* that was big in our house. I remember seeing Jimmy Wakely and liking the way he looked. He was a cowboy and had this great big blond guitar. Later he teamed up with Margaret Whiting. Now when I listen to them it sounds pretty schmaltzy, kind of like a country Nelson Eddy and Jeanette MacDonald, but the outfits were great!

One of the most startling things I remember seeing on early TV was Johnny Cash. This is back about '56. Most variety shows had a big chorus line of girl dancers, like the June Taylor Dancers. They'd form a circle and would be shot from above. The shows were big and glittery, with a cast of thousands like a Busby Berkeley movie. Right amongst all that Johnny did "I Walk the Line." It was really stark. There was his face, behind him only shadow. Way back there you could see one guy going *plunk, plunk* on a guitar, but most of the time it was just Johnny, shot from the side like someone on Mount Rushmore. I just sat there with my mouth open because it was so powerful. This wasn't the June Taylor Dancers. This was dark. Strong. And this guy—whoa. Commanding.

Hank Williams I loved, of course. I'm sure I heard about him as a kid, because I remember "Jambalaya" and "Kaw-Liga" almost as nursery rhymes from the early fifties. But the moment I actually became aware and curious about Hank was when I bought the Jerry Lee Lewis single "Great Balls of Fire." When I turned the record over there was a version of "You Win Again" that is for the ages. One of the all-time great rock and roll songs. And there, just under the title, it said, "Hank Williams." I had to learn about that guy, so I began to find more and more great music by him. Songs like "Lovesick Blues," "I'm So Lonesome I Could Cry," and "Your Cheatin' Heart" just slayed me. Hank became one of my biggest influences and is still up there on the mountaintop.

Another at the top of my country list would be Lefty Frizzell—I always wanted to record a version of "Long Black Veil." I loved Webb Pierce. There are many great songs, but it's enough that he did "I Ain't Never." Whoever played that guitar...! I recorded that on my *Blue Ridge Rangers* album. I loved Chet Atkins. He was such an inspiration. I don't know if any musician ever practiced more hours than Chet. Ever heard "Yankee Doodle Dixie"? That's pretty doggone advanced. The guy had all his fingers on both hands working. There's been a couple of those guys in the history of the guitar. It must have taken thousands upon thousands of hours of practice. Or maybe there's another race of humans that are wired differently. I used to wonder if that wasn't true, because it took me such a long time to develop as a player. But then there's always the question about how much you can learn versus how much you have inside of you.

Merle Haggard is one of those artists who hit me really hard way back when and continues to have a profound influence on me all these years later. I guess it starts with that amazing voice of his. But through the years he's just made so many great records. Then there's the writing. Merle has such a thoughtful, intelligent, humble, fun-loving, badass view of the world! Truly one of the giants of music. I think it's not an accident that so many of these guys that I listened to are great writers.

As a teenager, I heard an awful lot of Buck Owens on the radio. "Tiger by the Tail." "Together Again." "Crying Time." Those records were very important to me. That twang, that energy. Don Rich, playing all that Telecaster. When the Beatles covered Buck Owens with "Act Naturally," that was not odd to me. George Harrison's whole style, playing hybrid with his fingers—listen to "Help!" That's a country guy. There was good pickin' in there.

I didn't really meet Buck until kind of by accident at the Bay Area Music Awards (a.k.a. the Bammies) one year in the eighties. He just showed up in a country sports coat and a cowboy hat. We got to be friends. He gave me one of his red, white, and blue guitars. Buck melted me when he told me that Don Rich really loved Creedence.

All this time, while I'm listening to blues, rock, and country, the folk music boom—some called it a scare—was building slowly all through the fifties, starting way back even before the Weavers and Pete Seeger. All this stuff was bubbling in coffeehouses, and then the Kingston Trio did "Tom Dooley" in 1958, and it just took off. There were a lot of folk hits during that time, so they started having festivals, which my mom so kindly took me to. When I asked her later why she didn't bring my older brother Tom, she said, "Oh, he wouldn't come." I was at the right age. I was twelve and Tom was sixteen, so Tom was into girls and cars, and hey, I was...serious.

The folk festivals on the campus at UC Berkeley were put on by a wonderful guitar teacher, Barry Olivier, who also gave me my first guitar lessons. I saw Pete Seeger, Jesse Fuller, Mance Lipscomb, Lightnin' Hopkins, Sam Hinton, Alan Lomax—these weren't just concerts: they were an education. I was enthralled by the whole thing. These folk festivals were hugely rewarding—just bedrock for me. And not just musically. I'm certain that folk music has a lot to do with my entire belief system in terms of how the world should work.

In the daytime, the festivals would offer many different workshops. Pete would talk about the style of banjo he was playing, or things like how a lot of the bluesmen such as Lead Belly liked the Stella guitar because it was built so stoutly. Pete Seeger spoke with such affection and reverence—and Pete had film! Of Lead Belly! I mean, oh my God—I'm seeing Lead Belly playing this big ol' Stella twelve-string, and then five minutes later Pete picks up a Stella, puts on some finger picks, and plays "Midnight Special."

I'd heard my mom sing "Goodnight Irene" way back when I was little. Watching a film of Lead Belly doing it—well, it sounded like what I was hearin' on the radio! Like Muddy Waters or Howlin' Wolf, except *they* had drums and electric guitars. But at these folk events it was almost like, "Shhhh, don't talk about that." I was learning about the folk police. They didn't like any commercial stuff. After "Tom Dooley," all the folk purists were raggin' on the Kingston Trio—"Who are *they?* They're just some college kids. They never picked cotton!" Gee, they took a song and *rearranged* it, and that's a bad thing? You mean like, uh, Lead Belly doing "Midnight Special"? I tucked things like that away in my brain. The folk people were just in their own little world. They didn't want to acknowledge Gene Krupa.

Seeing Lightnin' Hopkins was incredible. He had this huge hit, "Mojo Hand"—one of the coolest records ever made. It had that secret, forbidden, cultish thing—stuff that's just really hidden from the white man. I had to pay attention and try to figure it out. A mojo hand was actually a monkey paw. Whoa! I actually met Lightnin' Hopkins at the folk festival. This was within minutes of meeting Pete Seeger. Lightnin' was very gracious. I gave him a little piece of paper and a pen and he made a very shaky-looking *X*. That was his autograph. If I had been an adult he probably would've said no because he wouldn't have wanted to reveal the fact that he couldn't write. I kept that piece of paper in the drawer with my socks for the longest time, but it went missing. But I can say that the memory is better than any piece of paper. I met Lightnin' Hopkins.

Pete Seeger is the greatest entertainer I have ever seen. An incredible musician. He'd be talking, telling a story, that skinny body of his rocking, and his head would go back and out would come "Michael, row the boat ashore..." You were there in the boat with Pete. Then he'd get everybody in the whole audience to sing along in three parts. It's like, "Damn. How did we all just do that for an hour?" I've never seen anybody else do that—ever. I've tried it myself a few times! I've witnessed the Franks, the Sammys, the Dinos, the Elvises, but Pete Seeger just had the magic, the showmanship. It was authentic and it was effortless.

And right around the time I'm watching him, the House Un-American Activities Committee was flailing Pete. He was taking a stand by saying, "I have the right to believe what I believe." And these kinds of thoughts and ideas were helped along through music. That resonated a lot more with people than a stuffy old speech, especially with some unsuspecting kid like me. There were people fighting and even dying for an idea that in the end actually was good for me? And if enough people didn't stand up and do that, I wouldn't get to be free? That really spoke to me.

I loved Pete. I learned so much from him. He liked to present songs that had ideas, but he never lost sight of just singing and having fun. There was the big folk music canon to perform, and it wasn't all doom and gloom.* So even though I was a rock and roll kid, I just ate all of this up and thought it was the best. Though I didn't realize it at the time, Pete's influence on me was probably greater than any of the rock and roll guys.

Folk, rock, blues, country—I didn't make distinctions, wasn't separating them. "This is R & B. This is country." I was young and open to all of it.

I'm still that way. Get me going and it's tough to stop. I haven't mentioned records like "The Slummer the Slum" by the 5 Royales, or "I Confess" by the Four Rivers. I covered that one in the eighties—had to lower the key. We can't do everything we want

---

* I had wanted to cut the Joni Mitchell song "Both Sides Now" with Creedence. I really loved that song and thought, "Man, with my style, a rock and roll band on it, that would be a really cool thing." Never got around to it.

to do. Only maniacs know that record, and yeah, I'm a maniac. That was a real dashboard-banger. Or "Henrietta" by Jimmy Dee and the Offbeats—that's a frantic rockabilly record. The Offbeats—that's just so wacky in the right way. Very punk name: "We suck! Ugh, stab me!" It was on Dot Records, 1958. The name, the label, the album cover, the sound, and the way the songs came in a certain order, on a certain side—all those little details were so important to me as a kid. They gave an album more mystery, not less. Pulled you in and got you hooked. It was all there to unfold, and that's one thing missing from music now.

Which brings us to Mrs. Starck's class.

In seventh and eighth grade at Portola Junior High, I was in Mrs. Starck's music appreciation class. There was some music history and some hands-on playing of instruments—rhythm instruments, mostly. I really, really loved that class. Mrs. Starck kept her hair in a ponytail and sported beads; she was slightly on the beatnik side, and she was amazing. We learned about Mozart and Beethoven—the idea that Beethoven was deaf was very intriguing to me—and even a little bit about boogie-woogie. Meade Lux Lewis and Albert Ammons—those guys. Mrs. Starck talked about all of it like it was important. Like it was real music, to be mentioned in the same breath as Beethoven. Which was way cool. We even learned some about the music business, how contracts were important and often unfair. I shoulda paid more attention.

One day, Mrs. Starck said, "John, you collect records. Why don't you bring some of your favorites, and we'll play them in class and you can talk about why you like them." I thought she was so cool for doing that. I know I brought "I'm Walkin'" by Fats Domino. I just loved Fats and how that record took its time. I'm pretty sure I brought "Boppin' the Blues" by Carl Perkins. I might've brought "Henrietta" just because I knew that it would probably make Mrs. Starck anxious. She was very tolerant.

Mrs. Starck was a great inspiration. Rather than thwarting me when I went over to the piano to bang out some rock and roll—which I'm sure sounded pretty awful—she encouraged it and acted like it was the coolest thing in the world.

My last class of the day was phys ed, right down the stairs from her classroom, so one day I just wandered back into her room. This was in the eighth grade. I don't know where I got the gumption to sit down and play. I think there was nobody around. I'm a pretty shy person, really.

Next thing I knew, there were a couple of kids standing there. I could do a few things I was learning at home: "Do You Want to Dance" and a couple of instrumentals that I was playing on the black keys in F sharp, kind of bluesy boogie-woogie. After a few days of doing that, there was a crowd of people. One day Doug Clifford was there. And he started talking about playing drums—he even said he had a drum. We decided to get together.

When I went over to his house, I saw a snare drum sitting on a flowerpot stand and a cymbal. That was it. Later, Doug got a hi-hat from a guy named Rich Knapp, who'd made it in metal shop. It was homemade, but it worked.

So we began to play. We started making music—me with my little Sears guitar and amplifier and Doug with his flowerpot snare and cymbal.

CHAPTER 4

"There's Somethin' Missing," Says R. B. King

I REMEMBER A TRIP to Montana with my father in the summer of ninth grade. I had my Silvertone guitar and I'd sit in the backseat of the car and play. I was trying out "Red River Valley" in a minor key, kind of making it blues or folk. My dad took note. It was so frickin' hot that the plastic pickguard would swell up like a melting candle. It must've been 115 degrees out, but I didn't care. I had my guitar and I was in a magical world, connecting with the shaman's secret path. I don't know how else to say it. I have the exact same connection to music today.

I came out of the womb whistling. I knew I wanted to express myself musically, that I had to, or else I wouldn't be whole.

The first guitar we had in the house was an old Stella built like a '48 Ford. Us kids used to play baseball inside the house, and the Stella was our bat! But I don't know if it was my dad's or my mom's, since nobody played it. My dad might've known some chords. By the time I was serious about it, my dad hadn't been around for a few years.

My mom and I would bring the Stella acoustic to the lessons with Barry Olivier and take turns playing it. Barry suggested a nylon string guitar, and that made things better. Learning music in a group, all adults except for me, two sessions of about six weeks each—that was a godsend. Barry was such a charismatic person and very sincere about it all. And I was a sponge.

Either my mom or Barry Olivier had told me to get ahold of *The Burl Ives Song Book*. In the back were a whole bunch of chords. "Oh, that's how you make a D chord?" That really helped a lot.

One night on our way to folk lessons my younger brother Dan was in the car. I played "S & J Blues" on the guitar. Dan said, "Wow, you're sounding *professional*."

We had an old piano in the house, so naturally I tried to play it. The piano was certainly out of tune. Sometimes I put tacks on the hammers to make it sound honky-tonk. I can't imagine a kid these days being patient enough to do that. We had a 78 of "Bumble Boogie" by Jack Fina. I played the record at slower speeds to figure out what he was doing. Slowly I learned, "Oooh, there's some mathematics to this." I just stayed at it and stayed at it until I could present a pretty plausible version of "Bumble Boogie." It was probably while I was in high school that I spent the most time practicing and playing piano. I never got real, real good with keyboard, although I could play "Great Balls of Fire" and "Whole Lot of Shakin' Going On." The intro to that song is still one of the coolest-sounding piano parts ever.

I saw jazz pianist Earl Grant doing "Fever" live on TV in 1958 or so, and I bought the 45. Little Willie John had done the song, and Peggy Lee, but as a piano song it was as fresh as "What'd I Say" and "Whole Lot of Shakin'." The song started with a cool riff. When the show ended, I went over to the piano and played it the best I could remember. I didn't know what key he was in, but I played it pretty much on the black keys, maybe in the key of B or F sharp. To get in between notes, he'd hit two notes—a trill or something. You try and hit a blues note—you can't bend a note on a piano. I hadn't heard that before. I had one of those orgasmic musical moments with "Fever." For an hour and a half I played it over and over and over, until I really couldn't reap any more emotion out of it. I was in another land.

Nowadays a kid could do it all on a computer, but way back in the analog world, you just sort of figured it out. A lot of early rock and roll was so simple guitar-wise that you could pick a song apart and learn how to play it. I was really learning from records— what a band did, what parts they played. It sounds obvious, but before this time in my life, when I really had my hands on instruments, the music on the radio was all just sort of coming at you. I had to learn what the mystery of it was, why and how the guy played certain notes.

I remember trying to play Ernie Freeman's instrumental "Lost Dreams." That drum just sounds so forceful. It could've been made yesterday. I had an electric guitar that Tom had rented at Leo's Music. I'm sitting at the piano, playing the melody with my left hand, hitting one or two guitar strings with my right hand, playing the backbeat with one foot on Doug's homemade hi-hat, obviously enjoying myself. It was a way to make that "Lost Dreams" sound, but it was *me* playing instead of listening to the record. Then, for an instant in time, I got to realize how, say, Jerry Lee Lewis must have felt when everybody told him, "Jerry Lee— you're just crazy! *What are you doing?*" That's exactly what happened to me.

I'm sitting there playing that song on three instruments and my mom comes in the front door and says, *"Oh, Johnny!* What *are* you doing?" Like, "You're just crazy!" I said to myself, *Yeah, okay. This must be right!* My mom wasn't wild about rock and roll. She thought Elvis was kind of crude. I think she wondered if it was respectable or not. One time she went to the Monterey Jazz Festival with a couple of girlfriends, and when she got home, she couldn't stop talking about a song one of the jazz guys did—"I think it was called 'Give Me One More Time.'" I didn't have the heart to tell her, "Mom, that was Ray Charles's 'What'd I Say,' and that was rock and roll!" But you know what? I was in the house, banging away on the piano, and she let me. She didn't second-guess it.

My brother Tom was four years older than me, so he was able to move in circles I was too young for. And that included being with musicians who were a little beyond where I was, talent-wise. "Do You Want to Dance" by Bobby Freeman—that song got absorbed into our Fogerty brothers mythology. It's a very simple record: just piano, some bongos. There might be a little bit of upright bass in there and some guitar, but that's all—there's no real drums. It's a great performance, a cool rock and roll arrangement. Plus Bobby was a Bay Area guy, and Tom knew the piano player, Richard Dean. Tom's voice sounded just like Bobby Freeman's, and for some reason we had a set of bongos around, so Tom would play the song on the piano and sing, and I'd play the bongos. Tom had been playing for a few more years than I had, us alternating at the piano every chance we could get, and I learned to do that song just like the record. Bongos are pretty easy, right? Tom would sing that song deep into the night, even at two in the morning, and as good as he was, our neighbor would object. It was cute.

Tom had a really sweet, mellow voice with a high range like Bobby Freeman's or Ritchie Valens's. He was perfect for that stuff. Tom could've been in the front of a white doo-wop group like the Crests or Randy and the Rainbows, singing something like "Sixteen Candles." At some point he hooked up with this band Spider

Webb and the Insects—older guys with a sax player. They came over to the house and did a song with Tom: the Ritchie Valens hit "Donna." I wish there was a record of that. I can still hear it in my mind—Tom singing, the sax player playing the guitar filler parts. Even my mom thought it was cool. The Insects brought these gals with them—rock and roll gals dressed alluringly in tight clothes, enhanced attire for men. Mom didn't like that, and she let the guys know afterward. Even being younger I could kind of tell there was something up with these chicks. My mom was embarrassed for me, I guess.

The musical times with Tom were really magical. I remember we were in his red and white '56 Bel Air station wagon a little later, when he was married and had a couple of kids. We're driving along and the riff for "When Will I Be Loved" by the Everly Brothers came on the radio, and we just looked at each other with that I-just-died-and-went-to-heaven look. We did that exact same move the first time we heard "Satisfaction." We're in the car and along comes that riff: *daaah daaah da da daaaa*... There was a lot of that sort of thing.

Tom and I both loved music, and shared it as brothers. I don't think Tom had much of a cross word for me then.

The inevitable course was to get an electric guitar and play rock and roll. When I was twelve or thirteen, I bought my first guitar at Sears—a $39.95 Silvertone Danelectro (with one pickup—two cost more)—and a $39.95 five-watt amp. My mom cosigned for me. I promised to pay with my paper route money, which I did. The guitar had a cardboard case with an alligator finish. Later I sold the Danelectro to a classmate for five bucks. I think he paid me. I should've held on to that guitar.

Once I had played around with a couple of chords, I guess I had enough gumption to risk embarrassing myself (even though no one else was around) by trying to play Jody Reynolds's "Endless Sleep" on the Silvertone. That's one of my favorite songs of all time, and one of those spooky records loaded with attitude—"Wow, 'endless sleep': he's talkin' about *suicide!*" There's that *bumm-mmm bummm bowwwm* on that record—it's the bottom note of the guitar's range, a low E that really can't go any lower. I deduced that the sound was made with either a whammy bar or a bass sliding up. I had neither of those but figured out how to hammer on an E chord. The minute I started doing that, it was, "Oh, that's like 'Endless Sleep.'" So I sat there in my house and played it. I did that over and over on the Silvertone for probably an hour, because for the first time in my whole life I had performed a song on electric guitar. It was like, "This is *workin'!* I like this! I'll just do it *again.*"

The Silvertone's public debut was at a Christmas program in the eighth grade, when Mrs. Starck allowed me to play a little backup on one or two songs. I can't remember what I played—something Christmassy. I recall a D minor chord and a G. At the time, it was revolutionary for a school to present a program for the parents where some kid got up with an electric guitar. But no worries, parents: I wasn't very loud yet.

That's the guitar I had when I met Doug. I'd go over to his house or he'd come over to mine, and we'd jam. I liked his enthusiasm. Doug had energy and he was likable. It was casual and easy—we both liked rock and roll. Economically, we were kind of in the same place, and his mom and dad split up at around that time, so he went through the same thing I did.

I could play songs like Roy Orbison's "Ooby Dooby" and the single's other side, "Go Go Go," and we worked up a repertoire. Sometimes I'd sing a little—"The Battle of New Orleans" or maybe "Hully Gully." I started thinking about other kids I knew who played—to fill out the sound! We finally settled on Stu Cook for piano. Doug knew Stu, and when I was playing the piano in

Mrs. Starck's class, he mentioned him. Stu was smart and liked the same kind of music as Doug and me. He didn't know much about piano at the time, but he was willing to learn. So Doug and I decided to try him out.

Doug, Stu, and I were all pretty clean-cut, mainstream. Stu was the only one who was wealthy by our standards. He lived in a house up in the El Cerrito hills. He had a rumpus room with a piano. And he had a dad at home. Stu's dad was a lawyer with a great big firm that represented the Oakland Raiders, amongst others. Doug lived down near where I lived, down in the flats. It was all kind of middle-class territory.

At El Cerrito High there were three fraternities: Delmar, the 49ers, and the Saxons. Delmar was very clean-cut, preppy. The 49ers leaned towards jocks. Then the third one, the Saxons— those were not only the greasers, but the naughty boys, the bad boys. By the time I was a junior, I was lucky enough to be asked to join Delmar—at that point I had straight A's. Stu and Doug were in Delmar, but there was a big scandal where Stu jumped ship and became one of the Saxons. Stu went and got a tattoo, which was pretty far-out in 1962. I think he later tried to get it taken off.

The thing that came up with Stu was that at some point he would get impatient. And he would get—what's the word?— *difficult*. Stu would get in a tither about stuff and be pissed off. I made a speech about it after it happened one day. We were down in Stu's rumpus room rehearsing, some idea came up, and he wasn't even willing to try it—"That's *no good,* that's not gonna *work,* blah, blah, blah." Basically, he couldn't play the part, so he was yelling at the part he couldn't play rather than yelling at himself for not being able to play it. Finally I said, "You're that guy on the sidelines at the football game who's not even gonna try. He's not the coach, he's not playing in the game, he's just some dude standing on the side going, *'That'll* never *work.* Why did you try *that?!* Man, this *stinks!'*" I made that speech more than once, because over the years, that was Stu. He was that guy in Creedence. Stu could get in somebody's face. I was too shy to do that—or too polite.

I came up with the name the Blue Velvets for our band. And I was the bandleader, although I say that kind of comically. When Doug and I were first talking, I remember thinking, *Am I joining his band?* Then, *No—he's joining* my *band!* Along the way it became very clear. I was steering the direction. I had more music in me. And I wrote quite a few instrumentals. The Blue Velvets were an instrumental band—that was the whole premise. Every now and then I'd sing something like "Hully Gully," but mostly we did instrumental hits: Duane Eddy, Bill Doggett, Link Wray, the Ventures, Freddie King, Johnny and the Hurricanes.

The Blue Velvets were just a trio—guitar, drums, piano—so it wasn't a band with a lot of oomph, but back then there were a lot of little bands that weren't really fully formed. Johnny and the Hurricanes had a bass player, but you rarely saw that at a local level. And besides, we were the only rock and roll band in our school. Doug, Stu, and I played together as a band all the way from the eighth grade right through high school. Nobody else had the bravado to do something like that—"We're a *band!*" We were really considered kind of cool, but also kind of strange. After the Beatles hit, there were a hundred bands in our school, but for now we were it.

I believe the very first time the Blue Velvets played anywhere was at a sock hop at Portola Junior High at the end of 1959. We might've done five instrumentals. I know we played at least one song I'd written—a slow song, kind of an instrumental version of doo-wop, with those kinds of chords. Another of the songs we played at that first gig was a song I heard in the car on the way to the sock hop—"Bulldog" by the Fireballs. I just heard it on the radio and then when I got to school and had a guitar in my hand, I said, "Just follow me. It's a twelve-bar blues." I'm not made that way, to spring something unknown on people, let alone my own band, but that one time we did it—at our first gig! I was fairly practical. I wasn't trying to show everybody I'm Duane Eddy. It was, "What's my function here? They're hiring me to play for a dance. I better play danceable music." That remained my directive over the years, even as I got on the big stages of the world. I went for music that made you shake your body.

As we kept playing, opportunities started to open up, and this guy, Bob—I cannot remember his last name—took the Blue Velvets under his wing. He was with the El Cerrito boys club. We got to do shows all over the Bay Area—places like Pleasanton, San Leandro, and Oakland—representing the boys club. Because we were kids, Bob would drive us and bring our equipment. He was a really good guy, and he helped us. I've never been able to track him down, but I wish I could.

So the Blue Velvets got great exposure and the opportunity to play a lot. It was good discipline. We worked up three, four songs and went far and wide. We were playing somewhere in Northern California when James Powell first approached me.

He liked my little band. He said, "Well, I'm gonna make a record and I need a band to play on it." I was only fourteen. Unlike some musicians, I was always driven. If something lands in your lap, you're supposed to say, "Yeah, man—I'll do it!" Right? Nowadays every kid can make a record on his iPhone. So it's not such a romantic notion anymore. This was, "Mom, we're gonna make *a record!*" This was out in the world, making a recording. Just to be able to *say* it! How cool is that?

James was a black guy and a pretty doggone good singer. I think he was about twenty-five or so. He had a song he wanted to record called "Beverly Angel," a classic doo-wop. Really cool song. And he had others—every song was a girl's name. We rehearsed. I don't know how many times he came to either my house or Stu's rumpus room. James knew a guy named Joe Jarros who had a little company called Christy Records. He was a small businessman, and on the side he had a tiny label—the innocent side of the old-time rock and roll record business.

We were basically backing James, but to do that right, we needed a bass player on the record. Now, they had a string bass in Mrs. Starck's music room. A couple of times she let me play it. Mrs. Starck had made chalk marks on it so I could see the finger placements and play whatever song she wanted. Hey, it's like a guitar, only bigger.

So I decided I'd play bass on James Powell's session. I couldn't use the school bass, but on my paper route there was an older fella who played bass in a country band. They had a weekly gig in Oakland, broadcast on local TV. I always loved when he was home because we would talk about music for a while, and he was always full of encouragement for me. A cool guy.

So one day as I was delivering the paper, I told him we had this opportunity to make a record. He responded, "The heck you say! Really?" He was enthusiastic, so I asked to borrow his stand-up bass. "Sure, man. If I'm not home, just come tell my wife. The bass is in the garage."

James had rented a trailer. A string bass is huge. That's why they invented the Fender Precision—so you didn't have to go through this! I show up at the guy's house, and he's not there. His wife looks at James, she looks at me—I'm just some kid with a paper route. I'm not sure she understood the situation, but she let us take the bass. Lord, we drove across the Bay Bridge, with that big string bass in the open-air trailer, to Coast Recorders in San Francisco.

We'd already made a little demo record with Tom at a place called Dick Vance Recording Studio. The room was so small we actually had to open the window so Doug could sit on the sill and play his drums. I think we cut two songs there, with Tom singing.

All we got was a shellac copy. The guy just cut it right on the spot, and that's it—that's the only copy you have. I know for at least part of the song Tom had to manipulate the volume control on my Silvertone so it could sound like a vibrato. I just played and Tom turned the knob.

But Coast was a real recording studio. We walked in and I saw Monk Montgomery, the brother of Wes Montgomery. Monk was, like, the first jazz bass player to go electric. I thought, *Wow, the big time!* Walt Payne was the engineer. Years later he was the engineer on "Susie Q" for Creedence. Doug, Stu, and I did the music with James singing, and then I overdubbed bass, which turned out fine. James also overdubbed harmony with himself—an advanced thing for its time.

"Beverly Angel" is not quite "Earth Angel," but it's close. It sounds pretty good. It's got a big echo and a real ending—it doesn't just fade out. "Beverly Angel" didn't sell any copies that I know about, but that record eventually got played on the radio. Feature that: I made a record with my band at fourteen years old—a record that got played on the radio. Even weirder, it was an R & B record, a black record played on a black station—my *favorite* R & B station, KWBR!

I was pretty proud. I mean, I didn't assume, "This means I'm headed to Carnegie Hall." But get this: Stu took electronics with Mr. Thomas at El Cerrito High, and the project was to make a radio. Well, Stu made his radio, and the story goes that when he first fired it up, "Beverly Angel" came wafting out. Can you imagine that? "Hey, Mr. Thomas—it's my record!"

There were some times in my life where I went along with the crowd and was dishonest. When I was about eight years old, a little group of us kids started stealing stuff out of stores—the five-and-dime store, the hardware store. Y'know, just walk out with

71

something under your shirt. Then we would try to sell the stuff door-to-door. Well, that's how we got caught. What's a little kid doing with a spatula he's trying to sell to some mom at her door? It still had the tag on it from the variety store. I was caught. Plus I was ratted out. This one kid, Billy, thought he was such a tough guy. He's the same one who pushed me over on my tricycle when I was about four years old. I rolled over. I was crying. Billy was that edgy, ornery, smokes-and-swears-a-lot kid—a bully. Billy ratted us out. Not so tough as when he pushed four-year-old me over in the crosswalk. That sure wasn't funny at the time. I hope Billy turned out okay.

There was a point when I would steal a record, take a 45. I didn't have what I perceived to be enough money, even though I had a paper route. I believe I had been in the record shop when I saw another kid steal a record. My eyes got real big—I think there was some thrill in doing it, although I hate to say that, and surely there was also some pressure to pull off this kind of stuff. I'm not saying this for bravado, and I'm certainly not happy to be saying it at all. But it's a part of my story from those times.

So here I was, stealing a 45 here and there. I had taken many singles over a period of a year and some months. And I literally looked at this one day and said, "Music is the thing you love. Why are you doing this? This is terrible. It's the thing you love most, and you're breaking your own strongest rule. You know what honesty is. What else do you have besides your word?" I was messing up the thing I loved, putting bad feelings and guilt all around it—to the point where I struggled with the idea of coming clean with the store so I could be free of this bad thing I'd done. But no, I never was that brave, I hate to say.

If anything came of it, I guess you could say I became a real stickler about honesty. To the point of silly things, like when you're driving, there's a roundabout in the road and you're sup-posed to go around it, but you *could* cut through it. My kids will be going, "Dad! Dad! Cut through!" And I'm like, "Nope, even if it hurts! The sign says this way."

Because it's a slippery slope. One day you do that little thing, and the next day...Obviously, none of us is perfect. As you may have guessed, I'm a fallible human being. But honesty is still very important to me. The idea of being truthful. Moral.

That wasn't the only experience that made me this way.

In eighth grade I stayed home from school. My mom stomped on the furnace grate— "Oh Johnny! Wake up!" —and off to work she went. It was October of 1958 and the World Series was on. "Wow, I'd kind of like to see the World Series." In those days, it was played in the daytime. So I stayed home from school. To watch the series and play my new Silvertone. And I stayed home the day after that. My mom wasn't around to know. Nobody was.

Weeks later I was doing my paper route after school when Mr. Noricaine, a phys ed teacher, went by in his '49 Ford, and I thought, *Oh, my day is comin'*. A few days later, I was busted. My mom confronted me. She'd gotten a call from the school, and after having lost so many credits that year, I got four Fs and a D minus. I used to tell people, "That's what I get for concentratin' on one subject."

So I was in trouble, and deep. I had to go to summer school— twice. The second time was my last hope if I wanted to graduate with my class. Kids don't quite get what the consequences are until the consequences are due. Summer school this time was over at Richmond High—not even my own school. But whoa, there was Mrs. Starck, my music teacher from Portola Junior High! Rather than being a punishment, summer school was a revelation. It was great to be there!

And there was this girl in class. I never really knew her real name, but everybody called her Plookie. She was kind of a heavy-set black girl, and Mrs. Starck allowed her to bring her music to school. Plookie played a Supro guitar through a Supro amp with vibrato. Plus someone played tambourine. Plookie and a couple of her friends did some gospel stuff, and it was *so* good. She might've known only one or two more chords than me, but it was more about attitude.

This was the music I listened to on the radio, but I didn't know anybody doing it firsthand. I'd hear this spooky stuff like the Staple Singers, and I'd sit down and try to do it, and it would come out like the Ventures. Plookie had that thing, she had that sound, and she was...great. Absolutely great. And she was my age! This was really an eye-opener. Because instead of being way off in the clouds, something I dreamed about down in my little room, this was something tangible, right in front of me. It pointed me in a direction towards something I could do, rather than being forbidden, or being too dangerous for my mom, or being too embarrassing to attempt. It was, "This is what I like. This is what I'm gonna do."

Plookie took the time to show me what she was doing with the vibrato, and her cool amp. I had a dinky little five-watt amp, and hers was probably twice as big or more. So I got myself a Supro guitar. First an Ozark model and then a top o' the line Res-O-Glas from the Sears catalog. That Ozark was my main guitar for years. I got short-scale guitars because I thought my hands were small, and I noticed that I could really just bend those strings by putting light-gauge strings on my little Supro.

The light-gauge string thing started when Tom and the Blue Velvets had some band pictures done at a little photo studio in Oakland. They were moody black-and-white pictures, and we were dressed up in suits. Just sitting there at the photo shoot was a Stratocaster guitar. It had that sunburst look and was all curvy. For a long time that was the only good guitar I'd ever held. But what really caught my eye was the fact that it had slinky strings, lightweight and really bendy. Like rubber bands.

I picked it up and went, "Wow, what's goin' on here?" I was

using Black Diamond strings, and positioned in their normal places they're pretty rigid, taut. Holding that Strat just made me think, *How can I do that?* So I would go down to Louis Gordon Music and, along with my normal set of strings, I would buy an extra high-E string. I would put the first E string in its normal first-string position. Then I'd put the other E string in the second-string position and move all the other strings down one spot lower than intended, making them all lighter gauge.

Later I found out that James Burton did the same thing, but he was using a banjo string for the high string. I didn't have enough knowledge for that move. But fairly early on I was into the light-string thing. It was a fortunate coincidence that I picked up that Stratocaster. It showed me that I could really just bend the heck out of those strings, which became an essential part of what I did.

Around the time we made the record with James, we would get together with Tom and do stuff. We were the Blue Velvets, his instrumental backing band. When I was in the ninth or tenth grade, we were at some guy's makeshift studio near Vallejo. It was the Blue Velvets plus Tom. He was singing. This guy had a couple of reel-to-reel tape recorders. Something was going wrong with his equipment, so we took a break. At one point he was fixing something on the tape recorder with a crescent wrench. Like a guy from an auto shop working on audio equipment. It was funny.

I don't know where Tom disappeared to. Stu went off to buy some smokes and Doug went with him.

"John, you wanna come?"

"No, I'm gonna stay here."

"Why?"

"Because I might learn somethin'." How often do I get to be at a recording studio?

So I'm just watching this guy with his wires. And he says,

"Y'know, when you're recording this stuff, remember: it's kind of like a glass of water."

"Huh?"

"You guys are making all this racket, but you're gonna have to put the singer on there."

"Yeah, okay."

"And you gotta put the lead guitar on there."

"Yeah. You mean it's like, 'Is my glass half empty or is it half full?'"

"No, no, no—not that way. You got a glass of water—that's your record, the thing you're trying to capture on tape. Remember that you can only fill the glass with so much water. After that, it all spills out. It's not going to be on your tape anymore—it's wasted. It's a mess, and ugly things happen. So if you're going to have something at the top—like a vocal—other things have to be less, so it doesn't overflow."

Analog tape saturates in a beautiful way—the old blues records, Bo Diddley and Chess Records, rock and roll in the golden age, Manfred Mann singing "Do Wah Diddy Diddy." If you sit right there on the red and everything's calibrated right, that's where rock and roll lives. The great engineers learn how to manipulate that. We don't stop where it starts to go into the red—that's the holy grail.

Digital can't do that. When you're recording in the digital world, you're backing off from that, wimping out. It can't go into the red. To paraphrase that wise old guy, the glass is overflowing, and it's ugly. Digital breakup is not a pretty sound.

So what this guy taught me that day stayed with me the rest of my life. When the guys came back, they were snickering—"Well, did you learn anything?" Later I tried to talk about it. They laughed.

My bandmates didn't really desire to know that stuff. I had to kind of drag them along, kicking and screaming. Sometimes they were in it; sometimes they'd go off with a girlfriend or to a party.

And I was left there—"Oh. Yeah, okay." Stu actually told me a couple of times, "Well, music isn't my whole life!" In Stu's case, it wasn't. In my case, it was. I'd caught it, and it had caught me.

I was the guy who always wanted to learn. I thought, *I'm gonna research this. I'm gonna scratch at it until I can figure it out.* It was about *learning*—learning what it was and how to do it. This was way more mental than, "Oh, poor me, I can't do it because I'm in a crappy recording studio." The great thing about rock and roll was that most of it was coming out of garages on some little label that said Del-Fi or Sun. They were making not only okay records but *the best* records.

Even though we were all very, very young musicians, I was always ahead of the other guys musically—and therefore, right from the get-go, I was the guy showing them what to play. Doug kind of knew that the foot went on one and the snare beat went on two, but that was about it. It was up to me to really study songs on the radio, discern what people were playing, and how that worked within that arrangement of that song. I was the translator. I could decipher. Most other people just hear music as one big sound coming at you. When I heard music, I heard the parts.

Hearing music live went a huge way towards my understanding, and the shows I saw at the Oakland Auditorium were another big influence. Those big revue extravaganzas where each artist got a half hour—James Brown, Jackie Wilson, Duane Eddy, Ray Charles. At all the shows that I saw at the Oakland Auditorium I was in the front row. I was in the front row for every one. I remember standing in line with Doug and Tom—Tom was the transportation, the wheels. We would get down there at three o'clock in the afternoon and be the first ones in line, so when the doors opened a few hours later we'd haul ass and sit front and center. That's how I could see so much detail.

I saw James Brown when I was fourteen. There was such precision. He'd sing one song—"Please, Please, Please"—and then, suddenly, *pow!* James goes down on the ground with the splits. Then he's up on his feet and into another song. *Bam!* His legs are going crazy. Another song! *Bam!* He might've been on for twenty minutes, but he and the band did twelve songs. The idea was to explode in a very short period of time. Energy! At the end, everybody's mouths hung open—"Whaaaa happened?" I loved that.

Larry Williams jumped off the stage with his guitar, and all these girls surrounded him. *Bam!* When they pulled away he was naked to the waist. They had shredded his shirt. Jackie Wilson came out in a tuxedo and all the women totally lost it. White girls, black girls—didn't matter. Jackie was movie star good-looking, with moves that were graceful, effortless, like a panther. Deejay Bouncin' Bill, the emcee, came out and told the women, "You've got to get back in your seats, back in your seats," because of the fire marshal. With Jackie Wilson it just kept happening. The cool R & B backing band we saw there several times had a song called "Spunky Onions" (it had started out as "Funky Onions"), and the guitar player hit what I now know is an augmented chord. Tom turned to me and said, "You should really watch what that guitar player is doing." He wasn't telling himself that—he was telling me. I wondered about that later.

There was one show at the Oakland Auditorium that turned out differently than all the rest. As usual, we had gotten there in the afternoon so we could be first in line. Well, they opened the doors as usual at six or six thirty. Then we sat there for the longest time with nothing happening. The time for the show to start came and went. Still no word....By now the auditorium was full and everyone was ready for the show. It got later and later and nothing was said to the audience. People started to murmur and were getting a bit upset.

Forty-five minutes to an hour after showtime, there began to be a stirring coming from the back of the auditorium. As we turned to see what it was, a few guys came walking down the center aisle on the main floor. They proceeded to walk right past the front row of people toward the stage. A couple of guys had dry cleaning bags over their shoulders, and slowly the audience began to realize that these guys were musicians—part of the show. As they got to the stage—which was raised up from the floor maybe four feet— they each hopped up onto it.

The audience relaxed a bit, thinking that now the show would begin. One of the guys sat down at the grand piano and started to play the opening of Ray Charles's "What'd I Say," which was a current hit on the radio. When he got to the part where the right hand does a little break and then the verse-ending riff, he fumbled and couldn't do it. He tried that riff a few times but could not play it cleanly. Well, the other guys had gathered around the piano, so one of them pushes this guy off the seat and sits down and tries to play the riff. He also fails and gets pushed away by yet another "player." I think five or six guys had a go at it. Finally, I believe Bouncin' Bill—the emcee—came out and scooted them back-stage. Watching this scene, I said to myself, *This isn't right. It seems so amateurish.* I made a vow to myself that I would never let this happen at "my show." I was fourteen years old.

I believe it was later on in this same show when I got some more "showbiz instruction." Bouncin' Bill announced the next act, the audience cheered, and...nothing. No one came out. He announced them again, and still nothing. After a couple more times, Bill went backstage, and suddenly a whole bunch of guys came flying out onto the stage, all dressed in matching suits. Bouncin' Bill was obviously pissed at this bunch, so he went to the mic and said, "Somebody had a royal flush and he wasn't gonna come out until the hand played its course." That was another lesson—as in, "Gee whiz, don't treat your audience like crap—they've come here to see *you!*"

In spite of that, we saw a lot of good presentation, good professional showbiz at the Oakland Auditorium. What I learned at the knee of James Brown and Jackie Wilson was how to *entertain*.

My mother sent me back to Catholic school in the ninth grade—St. Mary's, where my older brothers had gone from ninth through twelfth grade. There wasn't a whole lot that worked out for me there, but they had a boys' glee club at St. Mary's. Now *that* was awesome. One of the songs we learned was "There Is Nothing Like a Dame" from *South Pacific*—"We got mangoes and bananas..."

When music is all you've got going, you cling to it. When I first started up at the school, the dean was this guy named Brother Neil. He let me know right away, "I had both of your brothers. I got an eye on you. I'll see you in detention." And he did.

After that year, Brother Neil ran off with the receptionist, quit the order, and got married. Some of my friends were getting hit on by this brother or that brother. We were kind of disgusted. For me it was another slat gone out of the white picket fence that is the Catholic Church.

At one detention I was supposed to write something a thousand times—some sentence like "I will not chew gum in class." Well, my pen ran out of ink. And in detention you're not allowed to talk. I couldn't tell anybody or get up or raise my hand. So I filled in all the rest with the empty pen. If you looked close at the paper, you could see the imprint of the inkless pen. The brother looked at it and said, "Are you crazy?" Of course, I should've known—back when I was born I had inherited original sin from some guy millions of years ago. I should've known that you'd better not run out of ink, right?

One time when I was staying after school, this brother, an older gentleman, had a talk with me. I was having a hard time in school, so coming to class wasn't necessarily something that made me go, "Whoopee!" So the brother was giving me this talk. Now remember, these are religious people. You're not really supposed to be talking about sex, except that you're dealing with teenage boys with absolutely raging hormones, meaning they may go twelve seconds without having sexual thoughts, if the thoughts haven't already knocked them unconscious. And at some point the brother asked if I thought about sexual things, and I said yeah. And he says, "Well, maybe your underwear is too tight." I sure remember that phrase. I don't even know how I responded. And I'm thinking, *Oh, here we go. I got a brother hittin' on me.*

Music—thank God. We had formed a little musical group at St. Mary's. Baynard Cheshire played guitar alongside me. Baynard had a little National electric guitar, and sometimes I'd swap and let him play my Silvertone. Ron White, a guy who could really play, was on drums, and John Tonaga played piano. I don't think we had bass. I can't remember if the band even had a name, although we might've made one up on the spot. I know I brought those guys over to play once at El Cerrito High.

When our little group played at St. Mary's, the principal was Brother Frederick. He was a little short in stature. (I only noticed because he seemed to be overcompensating. We learned the phrase "Napoleonic complex.") At the time, I had been listening to Elmore James, and he'd inspired me to learn a vibrato technique that involved holding down three notes in the key of E, like the high part in Link Wray's "Rumble." You just hit it once or twice, and shake like crazy to imitate Elmore's slide. So there we are in the gym at St. Mary's, playing some fast rock and roll instrumental, and I start doing that E thing. I'm shaking, and the sound is coming out *BEEEEEEEOOOOOOOOOW!* The kids are all digging the rock and roll. If you want to say "in a frenzy," I won't argue.

And suddenly it just goes quiet. Someone pulled the plug! I look up and there's Brother Frederick, frowning, and suddenly it becomes apparent that I have committed the sin of all sins, because my body was shaking while I was playing. I didn't even know! I still don't. It's rock and roll—that's what you do! Brother Frederick had turned it into plenary indulgence, Hail Mary perversion: "This insidious music is going to be the ruin of the whole school!" Right then I think I lost all heart for finishing out at St. Mary's. I thought, *God, this guy's such a jerk.* Right out of *Bye Bye Birdie*!

Halfway through the tenth grade they took me out of St. Mary's. I don't know if the school just said, "We don't want him here anymore," or what. But I was relieved. I got to start fresh at El Cerrito High. My grades and attendance certainly improved, but it took me a while to get my bearings. On my first day the biology teacher called on me to answer a question, so I stood up to answer as I had been trained at St. Mary's. There was sort of a murmur in the class. I sat down and the teacher said, "That's a wonderful answer—and by the way, you don't have to stand up here."

For a second I felt embarrassed, but then I looked over at this girl who was smiling at me in an unthreatening way. She was a cute girl with glasses, and she asked my name. I was like, *Wow, there's girls!* Everything was so friendly and easy. Man, I loved El Cerrito High!

When I was sixteen, having a car was definitely the thing. I wanted to get a learner's permit and a license, but my mom resisted. My older brothers had gotten tickets and she didn't want the hassle. I had gotten a job at a gas station when I was fifteen— Tom had worked there; I'm sure that helped—so I saved my money and finally, at seventeen, I went and bought a car and just put it in our driveway. And I said, "Well, Mom, I probably oughta get a driver's license now that I have a car."

It was a green 1948 Ford Fastback, forty-eight thousand miles on it. It was a great car—the upholstery was perfect. I'd bought it for a hundred dollars—I'd tried to talk the guy down to ninety. This car had a Motorola radio with a little electric motor that went *grrrrr* over to the next station when you pushed a button. I put in toggle switches so the radio would jump between my favorite stations, KEWB and KDIA (formerly KWBR). I wanted to build a hot rod and screwed the car all up by taking it apart. What I didn't know was now the battery wasn't charging, so I was forever in situations where the car wouldn't start. I'd have to push the friggin' car down the road and pop it into gear. Because of my own foolishness that car gave me some intense, interesting moments in life. I ended up selling it for forty bucks to a guy who worked at the gas station with me. He still owes me twenty.

My first real girlfriend was a straight-A student and kind of insisted that I be one too. There's nothing like that kind of girlfriend to give you incentive to turn into a good student. I was fifteen; she was a year younger. She left me for a guy named Fred. I had an old lady car; Fred had a hot rod—exposed engine, a lot of chrome. He was a year older than me. He was in auto shop; I was in geometry. I guess my girlfriend liked the rugged, rough-and-ready thing at that point in her life and said, "Yeah, I wanna be in *that* car." That was a harpoon in my side. Talk about a broken heart.

I put that teenage emotion into a song I wrote, "Have You Ever Been Lonely." You know how there are these little signs that there's something wrong, and there's some other guy who seems to be pretty friendly with your girl, and you're the last to know? I wrote that song on piano. It had a little of the vibe of Arthur Alexander's "Where Have You Been (All My Life)" or Ron Holden and the Thunderbirds' "Love You So"—Tom would sing that one and I'd play piano. I play a piano solo in "Have You Ever Been Lonely" that's in the same style.

We cut the song in 1961 for Wayne Farlow, who had a little

label called Orchestra Records. We had already done one single for him. The label said "Tommy Fogerty and the Blue Velvets." When we were rehearsing the song in my living room, Wayne said, "I can't hear the solo. Play it in a higher register." So I moved it up one octave. Now, we could've just turned up the solo when we made the record, but this gave the song a different character *and* it made the solo stick out from the rest of the music. That's called arranging, and it was very good advice—a lesson to keep in mind for the future.

Tom sang, Doug played the drums, and I played the piano, not Stu. I don't think he was on that one, unless he played— *brrrrring!*—that opening chord on guitar. When I was writing it, I sang it a little harsher than Tom did on the record, with a few more hiccups in the vocal. Tom sang it pure and sweet. It's still really cool. Mom liked "Have You Ever Been Lonely." That was a pretty good song. I actually sent away and got that copyrighted and joined BMI.

With hindsight, it's funny and pretty sad that way back then I somehow knew how to do this at sixteen.

Around the tenth grade I hooked up with Bob DeSousa, who ran a studio called Sierra Sound Laboratories in Berkeley. I just looked it up in the phone book. I called and said, "I want to get into recording." Bob let me come over, bring my guitar. And experiment. I had to take the bus to get down there, and it became a regular thing. Bob knew how to do slapback echo with a tape machine and he enjoyed trying to come up with sounds. I hung out at the studio quite a bit, got in a lot of hours of experience. A lot of it was fooling around. I'd bang around on the piano, trying to figure out where you mic it so it sounds good. I was Bob's guinea pig. Bob seemed pretty amazed that I was able to just jump in and add harmony parts to the background vocal parts and even a bit of guitar.

And he let me experiment with the equipment. The Blue Velvets recorded a little Floyd Cramer–type instrumental called "Happy Little Thing" there. I think Doug Clifford named that one. And a guitar instrumental called "Bittersweet." I also remember a mournful instrumental called "Last Man on Alcatraz"—the idea being that the prison forgot about one of 'em when they closed the place down. Once Bob saw that I could play the piano a little bit, he even hired me for a session or two as a country guy, playing Floyd Cramer licks. I really liked Bob because he didn't look down his nose at me, all of sixteen years old.

Given how into recording I was, you won't be surprised to learn that I had been fascinated with tape recorders from an early age. Bob Carleton and I were a little team in grade school. We had started out imitating Stan Freberg records, lip-synching "Christmas Dragnet" for our class, one of us in a trench coat and hat like a cop, the other playing the interviewer. I still remember the words to that. In 1956, Buchanan and Goodman had this comedy record, "The Flying Saucer," where they told a story intercut with little bits of rock and roll hits. To do some stuff like that, Bob and I used this Wollensak recorder that Tom had brought home. One skit was called "The Daytime Ghost." The ghost was out of sync with Halloween because he appeared in the daytime. Bob and I wrote the story together and chose the songs. We both knew our records, but I was that kid who knew every line of every song, and I did all the talking.

I got a Sony add-a-track recorder in the tenth grade. It allowed you to overdub onto the original track. I had spent the previous summer babysitting my .younger brothers at my dad's house in Santa Rosa to buy the recorder, which I had seen at Louis Gordon Music. My dad reneged on the deal, and you can bet I was really angry about that. But if he wasn't going to help, I was going to do it the right way. I think I finally bought it with paper route money.

Les Paul had inspired me with his overdubbing. On his recordings where Mary Ford was the singer, she harmonized with herself. Sometimes she harmonized with a whole vocal group: on "Vaya con Dios" or "How High the Moon." Mary was the vocal group; Les was the band. They sounded amazing.

The Sony add-a-track was a gray-tweed-and-vinyl-covered thing. It was a revelation for me, since I could now capture what I was hearing in my head. I used it exclusively from then on. All through high school I'd be down in my bedroom recording. I even used the bathroom as an echo chamber. I spent hundreds of hours harmonizing with myself, and then adding guitar tracks. I learned an awful lot about what sounds rock and roll, what sounds true. I guess you could say that was the beginning of my one-man-band deal.

I managed to do a lot of recordings that were very much like the Ventures, with little harmony lead parts. I did folk songs, like "I've Been Working on the Railroad." I remember being down there in my room recording "Can't Help Falling in Love." We had a small house, and you couldn't do anything without everybody else hearing you. Mom later made a comment: "Gee, what is that you're doing?" "Oh, that's an Elvis song." "That's wonderful!" It was great to get some feedback.

In 1963, the Blue Velvets were playing a high school reunion for the class of '53. At some point in the night, we played "Green Onions." And this fellow comes up, R. B. King. He happens to be a black guy. I only make reference to this because there was a feeling—especially among white kids—that the more soulful stuff came out of black people. And he starts talking to us about "Green Onions"—immediately after we played it, I think. This is

only worth mentioning because what he told us was the truth—
the truth like a glass of ice water in your face.

For years and years I have said that Booker T. and the MGs
were the greatest rock and roll band of all time. Obviously most
people are going to say the Beatles, but it's what R. B. King was
talking about: no one ever had it like Booker T. and the MGs. I'm
talking about soulfulness, deep feeling, especially in between the
beats. How to say a lot with a little: that's one rule that will
always work—in music, on records, on the radio. Was Steve
Cropper scaring Chet Atkins? No. But I daresay, between the two,
most people would want to be Steve Cropper, and we adopted
Booker T. and the MGs as our idols. Even after we were pretty
famous and selling millions of records. The solo in "Proud Mary"?
That's me doing my best Steve Cropper.

When R. B. came up, he got right to it and said, "Well y'know,
when you're playin' that 'Green Onions,' there's somethin' missing." He said that phrase two or three times—"somethin' missing." I'm thinking, *Well…we're young, we're just a trio, and of
course we don't play as good as Booker T. and the MGs.* He
didn't say, "You white boys *suck.*" But R. B. King, in his gentle
way, was saying, "There's somethin' in between the notes."

Allow me to explain. Compare the Hank Ballard and the Mid-
nighters original first recording of "The Twist" to the Chubby
Checker version.* Ballard's has that *feel.* Many years later, I sat in
with Hank in some New York City club after his induction into
the Rock and Roll Hall of Fame, and I mentioned to the bandleader

---

* Chubby Checker's version of "The Twist" is a great record, and I love
it. What Chubby had done was to "straighten out" the beat, making it
more rock and roll—and much more accessible to the masses. I was
thrilled to meet Chubby onstage at the Rock and Roll Hall of Fame ceremony in 1986. Chubby made it a point to say to me [about my Creedence
work], "Those are *your* songs…you should play those songs!" Chubby
Checker belongs in the Rock and Roll Hall of Fame. Now!

how the Blue Velvets could never pull off that rhythm. His face lit up. He said, "Oh—you mean sand and Vaseline." I thought that was the greatest way to put it. And that's what R. B. King was trying to tell me in the gentlest way.

Some people can play a shuffle and some people cannot. I hate to say it's as simple as a cultural or racial thing, but more often than not, it's the white people who can't do shuffle. I've found there are exceptions: Chris Layton, who was with Stevie Ray Vaughan, is one of the all-time great shuffle players in the world. And I'd like to think I've been able to do it pretty good over the years. So later I tried to explain what R. B. King was talking about to Doug and Stu—particularly Doug—and I used that phrase all through the evolution of the Blue Velvets: the shuffle beat. But it's so much easier to play than to explain.

A few years after the R. B. King incident, the night before I was going on active army duty for six months, we're playing at a club outside Sacramento—I believe it was the Trophy Room. I'm not in the happiest of moods. I'm fairly nostalgic and down, leaving the next day. Who knows what's going to happen?

We're about to do a song, and I turn around to Doug and I say, "Play a shuffle beat."

And he says, "What's a shuffle beat?" *What's a shuffle beat?* It was like I'd been punched in the gut. You might as well have said, "What's a guitar?" This was 1967. I had used that phrase—"shuffle beat"—since 1958. I was speechless.

I must say, I avoided shuffle like the plague for years and years and years, as much as I needed it around. I'd be in rehearsal with the Creedence guys, and there it would be again: the shuffle problem. No sand and Vaseline. Sometimes I'd get frustrated and angry, particularly at Doug. Young musicians tend to rush. If it's a fast song, they tend to get excited and be a half block ahead of the beat before everybody else. Or they drag, especially on slower, funky things. I could almost see the ghost of R. B. King going, "There's somethin' missing here."

There's a couple of times when Creedence did play a shuffle beat more or less pretty good. One was our cover of "Before You Accuse Me." It's not Bo Diddley, but for some guys from El Cerrito, it's pretty good. We did this little two-sided narrative for the fans called "45 Revolutions per Minute (Part 2)," and it included a song in the background called "Thank You, Mr. J" that had a shuffle beat, and that was pretty tight.

I was pretty hard on Doug. I still am. Timing. In the eighties I was hunting up in Oregon. This was long after Creedence had broken up. And I had this dream. Our tent was on Miller Creek, and to get across it, you had to step on a path of rocks and logs— otherwise you'd land in the water.

So in my dream the rocks are representing the beats in music. I'm in the woods with Doug Clifford, and I step on all the rocks and get to the other side of Miller Creek. Then here comes Doug, *ker-splish, ker-splash,* missing the rocks and stepping in the water.

And I'm going, "No, no, no, you step *on* the rock. *On* the beat." And I woke up. My dream was about timing. About being on beat. There was so much of not being on the beat in the early days. What I'm trying to get at is, all was not lost, but it took a ton of effort, a ton of persistence, to get there.

CHAPTER 5

The ... Golliwogs?

MY SENIOR YEAR I almost didn't graduate. My job at the gas station really interfered. Somehow I scraped through. I had been accepted at the University of San Francisco but didn't have the money to go there. Contra Costa College, a community college, was the only road that looked open—to me, anyway—grade-wise and money-wise. I followed the crowd from El Cerrito High to Contra Costa College, those that weren't going off to Stanford or Harvard or anywhere else.

At some point in my life, I thought I might somehow pose as a history teacher. I still love history. But I hadn't even set junior college up to be very good, and it wasn't. I wasn't pushing, fighting to be there. When you're young, you need assistance and advice, a little nudge to get going. You can't just sit around and stare at the wall. I didn't really get guidance. I didn't even have it together enough to get the official dropout W, like you're supposed to, so it doesn't count against you. I just stopped going.

That's why I try so hard now to help my kids. One of my boys is at the University of Southern California, and another is at CalArts. I say that with a lot of pride. They're succeeding in a world where

I didn't. (Shane has since graduated from USC and Tyler will graduate in the spring.)

When I say things like this, my wife, Julie, grabs my hand and goes, "I think you did okay, John." But to me? Some big part of me still feels unworthy. Feature that. Wow.

In March 1964, the local PBS station ran this special, produced by the *San Francisco Chronicle* music critic Ralph J. Gleason, called *Anatomy of a Hit*. It was about Fantasy Records, a dinky little company in the Bay Area having its first hit record despite having been in business since the forties. It followed the rise of Vince Guaraldi's "Cast Your Fate to the Wind," which I loved, and this was a look into all the personalities involved. This TV special was in three installments running a week apart, so there was time to talk and think about it before the next episode. Tom and I considered Fantasy a jazz label and didn't think it would be a place that we should even knock on the door. But after seeing this program, we talked some more, and I decided, "Well, I'm just gonna go over there."

San Francisco was always a bit of a mystery to me as far as navigation. I was eighteen years old, and I'd probably gone once or twice by myself and had been there a few times with my mom. That was the big city, and you didn't just venture over there casually, even though it was only across the bridge from El Cerrito.

Once I found the address on Treat Avenue, I pumped myself up and went over. I pressed the buzzer, went up a little flight of stairs, and there was an office with a counter and some machinery and a typewriter, and somebody standing there talking to one of the guys I'd seen on the TV show, Max Weiss.

I had some manners, so I waited. I listened to the guy talk about all his big songs and all the places he'd been, dropping names like Johnny Mathis and Andy Williams. And Max keeps saying, "All right, Colonel…All right, Bright Eyes." And I'm thinking, *If you know all these people and they're all into your songs, why are you standing here?* It sounded like common show-business puffery.

When the other guy left, I introduced myself. And somewhere in the next ten minutes, Max called me both Colonel and Bright Eyes. He did that for the rest of our relationship. It was his way of treating the high and mighty and the low and full of it equally. Max was the resident hipster. He had a beard and sometimes wore funny Russian hats. I think he even had a fez. I guess I thought of him as a beatnik. Three Weiss brothers owned Fantasy: Max, Sol, and Milton, the bookkeeper. Saul Zaentz was the sales manager then.

Max took me into another office and listened to some of the instrumentals that I had brought. After three or four, he said, "Do you have any songs with words?" I'd been writing songs with words since I was eight. So I said, "Well, sure!" Max said, "Songs with words do a lot better than songs that don't have words." And he opened up a copy of *Billboard*, and the first five songs on the chart were all by the Beatles. (Yes, it was *that* historic week in April of 1964.) So we made another appointment, and I came back with songs with words.

We started recording songs for Fantasy Records. Later we signed a contract with the label in a very dark and noisy Italian restaurant. I couldn't read the menu, let alone the contract. I was underage anyway. All of us were, except Tom.

I also worked at Fantasy as a shipping clerk. I had to box up the records and call a delivery service, and a big truck would come and take our three boxes of albums. Maybe three hundred records a week were going out that door. It sure wasn't a lot. They had a shed with all the album cover stock—people like Mongo Santamaria and Korla Pandit. Fantasy clearly didn't have a clue about rock and roll. I know we went to lunch with Max a few times on

Saturdays, and he'd write down on the check "Vince Guaraldi." I think it was a tax write-off.

Fantasy had an R & B label called Galaxy, with songs like "Part Time Love" by Little Johnny Taylor. Little Johnny struck me as one of the old-fashioned stars—he'd call Saul Zaentz "Mr. Saul." Rodger Collins, who had the hit "She's Looking Good," was more my friend. Rodger was an entertainer. He'd make a guitar talk like it was asking a question. He played a Strat and had a Fender Super Reverb amp that was big and loud. He was a guy I was watching, because he was further along down the path than I was. I heard his record at the rifle range when I was in the army. To jack everybody up, get them happy about shooting targets with real bullets, they'd put on "She's Looking Good."

Fantasy recorded us in this lean-to out back. A big, open room. I think it had been a storage shed in the past and was connected to the main building. The tape recorder was right next door, in the warehouse where they kept the record albums. The doorway between the tape machine and the lean-to was a strange deal. They had cut out a hole in the drywall about the size of a normal door but had left the wooden struts, the frame, in the open space. It was explained to me that they would have to pay higher taxes to have a real door there (I have often thought about that syndrome— either you're in it or you ain't...). Because of that cheap-ass attitude, we were forced to squeeze between the two-by-fours with our instruments. There were no windows and you couldn't see the engineer—you just yelled. We kind of ragged on the whole setup. I remember recording "Fight Fire" when Doug was playing the maracas and hit the microphone right in the middle of the take. Things were just so funky.

By early summer of '64, we had recorded some songs. Max, the mad Russian, acted as our mentor and our engineer. We had all just graduated from high school, and Stu wasn't there for those sessions. I don't know how many songs we recorded, but we ended up concentrating on two of them: "Don't Tell Me No Lies" and "Little Girl (Does Your Mamma Know?)." Tom was the singer then. I remember overdubbing some tambourine and some tuned-down guitar that was supposed to sound like bass since we had no bass player.

Tom and I cowrote the songs, like nearly all the songs that came pre-Creedence. We hadn't joined forces as songwriters until after Lennon and McCartney. Before that, if he wrote a song, it was his song, and if I wrote a song, it was my song. On "Have You Ever Been Lonely," the writing credit is "Johnny Fogerty." The Beatles hadn't happened yet. Then we both got the idea: "Oh yeah—they write together." Tom's writing alias was Rann Wild. I really liked the singer Dobie Gray, who had the hit "Look at Me," and I liked the name Toby, so I became Toby Green. We were Wild and Green—songwriters.

Rock and roll was in a weird place before the Beatles came along. I had gotten so disenchanted, hearing the Singing Nun or the fifteenth rehash of "Can I Get a Witness," and I'd gotten restless down on the farm. So much so that around Christmastime in '63, I was down in Oakland, shopping, and I realized, "Oh my God, I'm listening to KSFO!" That was the "easy listening" station: you'd hear John Gary crooning "Once Upon a Time," and then they'd play Bing Crosby. Early that year, in May—I think it was on KFRC—I heard this song, "Please Please Me," by the Shields—at least that's what I thought they had called them. I heard the song every day after school for a week in my senior year, driving to work at the gas station. I thought, *Yeah, that's pretty cool.* Then they turned the record over and played "From Me to You"—*dahr dahr dahr dahar dar dar.* I was gone. I went, *God, what* is *that?* That record killed me. Then they disappeared. Nothin'. All gone.

The next January, suddenly they're playing the Shields all over the radio. They're gonna be on Ed Sullivan. It's not Elvis: it's a group, a whole band, and by now I know what they're really called. And girls are screaming for a . . . band? I was eighteen when that happened. I thought, *Man, this is the coolest,* and went down to the store and bought every record with "Beatles" on it. They were seamlessly going from this music to that: Arthur Alexander, Carl Perkins. People forget that part. They were coming from the heart of rock and roll.

I can tell you I didn't feel jealous — "Hey, they're taking our music!" We needed a shot in the arm in the USA, and they were shaking things up. That whole burst of energy. All of a sudden there's all these people who are really, really good. One after another: the Stones, Kinks, Searchers, Billy J. Kramer, Gerry and the Pacemakers. Remember: two months before January of 1964, Kennedy had been assassinated. When JFK died, it really punched me in the gut. I loved the Kennedys — all of 'em. For all their very human failings, it seems to me that they wore their wealth and their position of power in a much different way than almost anybody else that's ever been powerful and political. They had ideas that were very much for the good of the common man, and for the good of America as a society. And it cost them all very dearly. I was in the lunchroom at Contra Costa College when they announced Kennedy's assassination. I was stunned, in shock. Then here comes the Beatles. Thank God for the Beatles.

Put it this way: there were some little shows I did — with my band or just with pickup guys at a party — where I'd actually wear a Beatles wig and do three or four of their songs. I remember some older person saying, "Tell John he doesn't need to do that," as if I was going to be an Elvis impersonator for the rest of my life. It was fun, because *they* were fun. Quick, instant, like sea monkeys — put the wig on and "Yeah, yeah, yeah." We knew all their songs, and songs they never did, because you could kind of do 'em like the Beatles. I was, as you'd say, totally down with it.

*   *   *

A lot of things happened while we waited for our Fantasy single to come out. At this point, the band was not really meeting all that often other than for recording. I don't know how many times I played with Doug and Stu in our high school senior year—once, maybe twice. It wasn't a lot. At some point, Doug and I did a spate of frat parties. That was just for fun—half the time I'm sure the music wasn't very good because Doug and I were drunker than skunks.

When we got to the frat house to set up, the frat president would always say, "Hey, we wanna hustle the chicks, so you guys keep it slow. You just keep playin' slow songs."

"Oh, you mean like 'In the Still of the Night'?"

"Yeah, perfect! Like that!"

Right. Then we'd start, and maybe in the first half hour we'd play one slow number. After that, no more slow songs. Nobody really wanted that. We'd play "Wooly Bully," "Wipe Out," "Louie Louie," "Money," and "Twist and Shout" over and over. That's what they really wanted—a big, drunken howl. Doug and I had a running joke at those shows. As one of us was coming back from a pee break, we'd surprise each other with the house fire extinguisher. *Blam!* It would be all over me. I'd look like a flocked Christmas tree.

That summer of '64 I went up to Portland, Oregon, with Mike Burns and Tom Fanning, who were both in architecture school at UC Berkeley, and stayed there for about a month. I had met these two earlier that year, and I believe we had played a couple of parties together. They were great guys and good musicians, but I think they were on a career path to design buildings. Mike had the idea for us to go up to Oregon, audition a couple of local musicians, and get a job playing music for the summer. We ended up getting a gig at a club called the Town Mart. Mike named that band the Apostles. He had these beige shirts made that had big puffy sleeves—vaguely British Invasion–looking—and we had longish hair. In fact, when we got to Portland that summer, we walked into a diner and it was like we were terrorists. We were just going to sit down at the counter, get some pancakes and bacon. Except for the jukebox, you could have heard a pin drop. Then the jukebox stopped, and you could hear people saying, "Oh, they think they're the Beatles. Look at those juvenile delinquents!"

Mike played Farfisa organ. That was my first experience being in a band with one of those cool things. I was a real fan of that cheesy organ. "She's About a Mover," "Do Wah Diddy Diddy," "96 Tears" by Question Mark and the Mysterians. That song is one of those oddities—it's really awful *and* it's really cool. It held both positions! What an awesome song. Mike and Tom were really fun to be around—really good guys.

Portland was just an adventure. I liked the Northwest bands. The Sonics I loved. "The Witch"? I'm *still* going to do that song one of these days. Hell, yeah! We saw Paul Revere and the Raiders—they were still up there, not big stars. One night we were driving down the street in the dark, drinking beer, and saw the Kingsmen loading their gear. We shoulda stopped. Somebody in the car went, "The Kingsmen, man," and I went, "Wow."

Mike sang a few of the songs, like "Louie Louie." He was also tone-deaf. Mike literally had to count "One, two, three, four. One, two, three, four" in his head to make the chord changes. That's what he told me, anyway. I was determined to work on my singing and evolved into being the main singer of that little band. I took the add-a-track recorder on that Portland trip. I could record a whole set on one side of tape at the slow speed. We played from nine maybe until two, and then went back to the house where we were staying and spent another three hours drinking beer and listening to ourselves on tape. I was concentrating on my vocal, really going to school on that, because I desired not to be lame. And y'know, what I heard so far sounded kind of lame.

I'd sung in different situations but never thought I was killer. I did "Hully Gully" once at a dance for KYA at the El Cerrito armory. I had a little harshness in my voice, and people said, "Oh man, that was really cool," but that was only two minutes and thirty seconds. Maybe I had to get away from home to be free enough to do it. I knew in my head what I thought I should sound like, but what came out of my mouth didn't match that. I wanted to have a tougher sound, like the guys who really had an edge: James Brown; Wilson Pickett—"I Found a Love"; the Contours—"Do You Love Me"; Don Gardner and Dee Dee Ford—"I Need Your Lovin'"; the Sevilles—"Charlena"; and, of course, Little Richard, the best singer in rock and roll.

That's where I was trying to go. Have that alpha thing. So after listening to the tape, I'd go back the next night and try to make my voice sound a little harder, a little more rock and roll. I'd say words funny, in my own style. I'd try to do a scream going into the solo.

Portland was also the first place where I played harmonica. We were going to do a number—"Louie Louie," I think—and Mike was going to play the harmonica. Remember: this is the guy who's tone-deaf. A moment came where I just said, "Gimme that thing! No, I can't play it, but God, it's got to be better than *that*." I was never Little Walter, that's for sure. But it was rock and roll. It fit the occasion.

When we came back from Portland, Mike Burns called with a gig at this place in Berkeley, the Monkey Inn. Since the drummer we had used in Portland stayed back, I convinced Mike to use Doug. It was a typical college crowd, mostly UC Berkeley students. They had shuffleboard, and sawdust and peanut shells all over the floor. Peanuts and a pitcher of beer—for five dollars you could have one heck of a night. And that's all I was being paid, anyway. I think we got twenty bucks—for the band, not apiece—and all the beer we could drink. So you know what we leaned heavy on.

Tom Fanning and I played guitar, Mike was on Farfisa, and Doug was on drums. That lasted for a few months, and then it just kind of dissolved. I convinced the Monkey Inn's owner that I knew some other guys who could play. This would've been about 1966. We were making our records, but we still weren't really hanging together. Stu was busy at college or busy at frat parties down in San Jose, and he didn't come up that often, or he'd show up late in our set. This is when my brother Tom came in.

We had started out the other way: with Tom playing piano or singing with that beautiful voice. But now I was trying to include my brother in this new musical thing—my thing. I had to broach it to Doug and Stu. The first thing one of them said was, "Well, Tom can't sing." In fact, they had both said that way back at Dick Vance studios, which might've been the first time we were all at a recording studio. I was sticking up for my brother. (What's so funny about this is that later they went the opposite way. They would make it me versus Tom, with both of them on Tom's side.)

This was the fragile way our quartet started. Slowly we were evolving into the template for a rock and roll band as laid down first by the Crickets, and then by the Beatles: two guitars, bass, and drums.* There's no odd man out, no singer that doesn't do anything but sing and play tambourine. In a band, four is perfect. It's an even square, a beautiful shape in geometry. It's not six and a half people, which is too many, or three, which is too small.

With the British Invasion, I was beginning to see that those bands had certain instruments, and it had to be a certain way. The Beatles, the Stones, and the Kinks had all arrived fully formed,

---

* Of course, the very first rock and roll band had this lineup—Elvis on rhythm guitar, Scotty Moore on lead, Bill Black on bass, and D. J. Fontana on drums.

with a bass player. They looked professional, and we just weren't. It's not going to be rock and roll if you go out there with a tambourine and a triangle and a fiddle. To be a real band, we needed a bass player. Up until then, Stu was playing piano. One night I said, "Look, I want you to get a bass. Just get a cheap bass" — I think he got a St. George — "and we'll grow up learning this thing together. I'll show you what to do, and when you master that, I'll give you more bass lines to play, and we'll get there eventually."

Once Tom was in, he started just playing tambourine. Besides Stu learning bass, Tom was learning guitar — he literally couldn't play a bar chord, so it all had to be cowboy chords. It doesn't take forever to learn how to play rhythm guitar in a rock and roll band. Later we could really laugh about it. At one of the early Monkey Inn gigs, this drunk guy was standing in front of the stage, and he looked up at Tom and his tambourine and screamed, "You're *useless!*" It was drunken affirmation, a badge of honor that Tom could stand up there and be useless.

There was a lot of beer drinking at the Monkey Inn. In the back of the bar there was a partial wall, and over the top of it you could see the people playing shuffleboard. And whenever we played "Blue Suede Shoes," a fight would break out. You'd see the light over the shuffleboard swinging back and forth. Then the bartender would have to run back there and get everybody calmed down. Until we played "Blue Suede Shoes" again. We did it for our own amusement.

Talk about formative places. There's a habit I developed at the Monkey Inn that I had for the longest time: singing to the side, away from the audience. I had this cheap little mic plugged into my guitar amp, so I could use it for my PA as well as for my guitar. Sometimes watching the people would make me crack up, so I would look over and stare at the wall, singing sideways into the mic. Even in Creedence, I'd go up to the mic and sing sideways like that. It took me a long time to break that habit.

I played my cheap Supro guitar at the Monkey Inn. I didn't have a very good guitar or amp. My equipment was not professional. But somehow I sensed that this little gig at a dumpy little bar was a great opportunity for the future. Rather than just enduring the time spent there or using it as an excuse to party, I saw it as a way to gain experience for myself—and more importantly, a way to transform my little group of musical tourists into *a band.*

Throughout my two or three years at the Monkey Inn, I was learning an awful lot about how to play in front of a live audience. How to talk to a crowd. How the music affects the mood and energy of the audience. If you played the wrong song, it could really deflate the atmosphere. But if you chose the *right* songs, it would make the place soar, and the feeling could be magical. I learned to string songs together, to "take a journey with the music." Ah, man, the power of rock and roll!

During my growth as a guitar player and while thinking about style, I began to wonder about what Lead Belly had done with a twelve-string tuned down to D. That was so amazing. It was just… *the sound.* Rock and roll guys learn to play the E chord pretty quickly. A lot of great songs have been in that key. The Lead Belly sound is a whole step lower than that. You didn't hear it very often. And still don't! And the key to that basically was a guitar tuned low.

In about the ninth grade, I bought a cheap twelve-string guitar and tuned it that way. An acoustic guitar—I think it was a Harmony. It wasn't amplified, so I got a special sound hole pickup—I think it was a DeArmond—a big fat thing, and I'd play maybe one song. I can't recall what, but I'll bet it was closer to Lead Belly than the Orlons.

By the time of the Monkey Inn, I was using that guitar as a feedback thing. I had a volume pedal. Sometimes it had a separate amp, and sometimes it was the same amp my guitar was plugged into, the idea being that I could step on the volume pedal and activate the twelve-string, which is just sitting there tuned to a D chord, or maybe just tuned normally but down a whole step. And it would start to feed back instantly, because there's a drum beating and all this resonant stuff going on. The volume pedal cranked it louder—*AooOOOooOOO!* It was in that rock and roll tradition: a hellacious cacophony of sound. Where people go, "What *is* that?"

It had that kind of effect, like in a Little Richard song where Richard lets out a *"WAAAAAAAH!"* just before the sax comes in. "Be-Bop-a-Lula," one of my favorite records, did that. There's a break and the drummer just *screams "WAAAAAAA!"* Much later, I learned that when Owen Bradley recorded that song, the band was making such a racket that they moved the drummer farther and farther away, and finally he was in the doorway, but they could *still* hear him screaming. Owen Bradley turns to the engineer and says, "Why does he have to do that?!" The answer: "Because he's fifteen years old!" And Bradley let it be that way. That's the thing in rock and roll: it's wacky, but it makes sense. Feedback was my way to plug into that.

I also invented my own fuzz tone with a set of World War II army surplus headphones. There were two earpieces, and each one could function either as a speaker or a microphone. So I stuck the two earpieces together, wrapping them in duct tape, tin foil, and a piece of my old flannel pajamas, and put this inside a small coffee can. I wired one to an "input" jack and the other to an "output" jack mounted on the can.

To make this work, I would plug my guitar into an amplifier with the output of the amp going to the "input" on the coffee can. As I turned up the amp, that headphone would distort like crazy. The other earpiece would act like a microphone, sending that distorted sound to the "output" on the can. I could then plug that sound into a normal guitar amp, and voilà: distorted fuzz tone guitar. I had that for three or four years. Nowadays you just plug into a box to get that sound, but back then it was a revelation (although I listened to "Walk on the Water" recently, and if that's what I used, it's pretty awful and shrill—I had nothing to compare it to then).

There was nothing like the Monkey Inn for experimentation. We could develop as a band and there wasn't a lot of pressure yet. We just had to present fun. They were having a fight back there anyway. I still chuckle when I hear "Blue Suede Shoes."

For the longest time, the single we recorded for Fantasy just didn't come out. It was a lifetime to us kids. Finally, in November of 1964, Max told Tom, "Come on over. We have your record." At that time we were still the Blue Velvets. Either Max didn't like "Blue Velvets" or, now that we were a quartet, he wanted a new group name. So we called ourselves the Visions, right? Which to me always sounded like that guy in "Earth Angel" who sang "da vision." As in math. So for, like, five minutes we were the Visions.

Tom, Doug, and I drive over to San Francisco. "Where's our record? Where's our record?" Max gives us a box of twenty-five singles. Now, we're expecting our new name to be on the label: the Visions. But we pop open the box and the label says…the Golliwogs. We say, "Oh man, somebody really screwed up here!"

Max tells us he didn't like our new name, the Visions. It wasn't interesting enough. So in a stealth, surreptitious move of intrigue, he had named us the Golliwogs. "We're trying to have you guys be like the British Invasion here. So we wanted to give you a hip-sounding name. Mod. It's mod."

"Yeah, Max, mod. Okay. But what is a golliwog?"

"Well, way back during a war that England had with some other country during the colonial British Empire days—"

"Yeah, Max. What's that got to do with us?"

"Well, the British soldiers would interact with the people of the country that they were actually trying to conquer. So the people in that country made these little dolls that had fuzzy hair and black faces—kind of like a voodoo doll."

"Oh, okay."

"The British soldiers got to calling these dolls wogs. Like a golliwog. And sometimes they even called the people golliwogs or wogs. So this little voodoo doll is a really important thing in British history. See, we want you guys to seem like you're British—part of the hip, British musical invasion!"

"But Max—we come from El Cerrito."

So we went home very disgruntled. And dozens of times later, we would find ourselves reenacting this rationale as we had heard it in Max Weiss's office.

"John?"

"Yes, Mom?"

"I thought you guys were the Blue Velvets?"

"Yeah, see, Mom, they named us after this doll..."

For the rest of the time that we were the Golliwogs, we had to explain the name to every single person that ever heard our music. And everybody's telling you, "Well, that's dumb!" So you might say it was a very self-limiting—and perhaps self-fulfilling—prophecy. If you have to explain a marketing device, then you're barking up the wrong tree. Kind of like Edsel.

We hated the name. We felt helpless. And our first single came and went. My goal was to somehow figure out how to be a great band and make a great record. Max was no help. I'd be at the microphone hearing all these things Max was telling us, things that were about as applicable as that Golliwog doll: "How about you put on a British accent?" Or "Put on a 'Yeah, yeah, yeah.'" Or "Get that sound on your guitar that George does." Just weird, from-left-field advice from an older person.

I was feeling frustrated. We were desperately trying to figure out how this works. And I'm realizing some of the shortcomings of our sound and our approach. At one point I remember looking across the microphone at whoever was there and saying, "Well, I guess Phil Spector's not gonna come down here and produce us."

What that really meant was, I'm going to have to figure out

what producing is. And do it. I was expressing it out loud. I said it for my compadres in the room. Because I was only pulling for the band. I never ever thought of myself any other way through all the years I was in it.

So after that, I was a producer. I didn't get credit for it, of course. Max got some kid and named him our producer, ha ha. But what this really meant was that I began to think of the finished record at the moment of conception. I learned to envision the sound of the instruments and the style of the arrangement as I was writing the song, sometimes letting that vision guide the writing process. This is quite different from how a singer-songwriter creates. Usually, the writer is preoccupied with words and melody and his focus is on completing the song. He leaves the record making to someone else.

This syndrome of recognizing a needed service or function — and then assigning that task to myself — happened over and over on our journey through showbiz.

I finally got to tell Phil Spector that story, by the way. In the eighties I had gone to one of the Rock and Roll Hall of Fame's secret inner sanctum meetings to try to get my hero Duane Eddy included. And who should happen to be sitting next to me but Phil Spector. I told him my Golliwogs story. He got a big kick out of that. As a matter of fact, two or three years later it was Phil who called to tell me that Duane Eddy had gotten into the hall of fame.

Tom sang lead on our first single, "Little Girl (Does Your Mamma Know?)," and I sang harmony with him on the other side, "Don't Tell Me No Lies." On the next single, "Where You Been," Tom sang the lead again, and on the B side, "You Came Walking," I harmonized again. We weren't quite good enough to pull that one off — with a little higher level of musicianship and a George Martin behind us, I think it would've been cool. One side of our third single was "You Can't Be True." The other side was "You Got

Nothin' on Me." I sang lead on both of these. They were bluesy, edgy—more like me. More like how I had sounded in Portland than this sweet, mellow thing that Tom was always doing.

I had never heard Tom sing rough. But by the time I had come out the other end of that trip to Portland, I wanted my music to have more of an edge, be more raw. There seemed to be an audience for a more bluesy approach to rock, and we kind of got into that— certainly the Stones had more of that. It was less doo-wop and a lot more growl from Mick Jagger and the boys. You'd see these other British bands, what they were doing—I thought we should follow that path, rather than bongos and tambourines. There seemed to be a model for us to grab on to and push forward with.

So I sang our next single, "Brown-Eyed Girl," and went in that direction. I just thought it was a much more viable style than that other Bobby Freeman kind of sound that we'd done with Tom, which I felt was dated, passé. "Little Girl," the piano, doing doo-wop…it just seemed old-fashioned. And when you're a kid, that's fatal—"Whew, that's *two years* ago!" I was trying to catch up… or get ahead!

"Brown-Eyed Girl" was a regional hit. It was big in California's Central Valley, starting in San Jose. And it enabled the Golliwogs to actually start getting some local musical dates. We'd work Turlock, Merced, Roseville, Modesto, Marysville, playing school dances and National Guard armories.

We'd have these jobs way up in the northern part of central California or way down south—Tom and me in one car, Doug and Stu in the other. Later we graduated to a Volkswagen bus that had been owned by the Du-All floor company—it was still painted that way. Our gig would be over at one or two in the morning, and we'd drive home in the night listening to Wolfman Jack on XERB. Wow, what great memories I have of that! Wolfman Jack was so great. He was broadcasting on a radio station from Mexico, and I guess the normal U.S. transmitter regulations didn't apply. His transmitter was something like 250,000 watts (or more), and you could hear that station all over the United States.* The Wolfman played R & B–leaning rock and roll, and it was presented with much urgency. Kind of like you were peeking into a hidden vein of music that no one else knew about. Records like "Mystic Eyes," "It's All Over Now, Baby Blue," and "Gloria" by Them; "Up in Heah" by Junior Wells; "You're Gonna Miss Me" by the 13th Floor Elevators; "Are You Lonely for Me" by Freddie Scott; "Keep On Running" by the Spencer Davis Group; and "Try a Little Tenderness" by Otis Redding. When he got really excited, the Wolfman would do kind of a pep-talk rap and then play the werewolf howl. It was frantic and *great!* Tom and I really looked forward to those rides home.

Now that we were doing some real concerts, we needed clothes. The four of us went somewhere, maybe the Haight-Ashbury. Max from Fantasy was probably there too. We were young people with no real experience buying clothes, trying to dress currently. And Max was telling us what was hip. In one store there were these big, shaggy, white fur hats—Himalayan yak hats. Hard to say now who they were for—women? Bald-headed guys? Sherpas? But we bought 'em.

When we'd come out wearing our big white hats, some would snicker and laugh. "Here's the Golliwogs!" We were *those* guys. Always going to be a local band. Later on there'd be a point of just ripping that furry hat off and throwing it in the audience, or at somebody. I think at least one of us threw his out in the audience. I know I don't have mine. Because I hated it.

---

* I sent away for a Wolfman Jack photo that you could iron onto a T-shirt. When it arrived I was disappointed. It was a cartoon drawing of a hipster wolf.

But something was working, and we opened for Sonny and Cher at the Memorial Auditorium in Sacramento. That's the place where Keith Richards got knocked unconscious when his guitar made contact with a wrongly wired mic. (When I stood in that exact same space, I always got shocked there as well.) Sonny and Cher were the big time: "I Got You Babe."

So we do our set, and by God, there's such cheering going on that we're going to get to do an encore. Outstanding! They open the curtain. We come out doing "Walking the Dog." We did it more funky, like Rufus Thomas. We're rockin' away when suddenly—*whoosh!*—the curtain closes again! *What?*

It turned out that "Walking the Dog" was Cher's very first number, the first number of Sonny and Cher's set. Ixnay! I'm sure it would've been all right—she's Cher and we're not. But no, they used the big hammer. Our moment was stolen from us.

How does a band survive that kind of crap? You keep on. Our ragged "Brown-Eyed Girl" was progress, a step up. "You Better Get It Before It Gets You"—I like that one a lot. "Fight Fire" was another. Man, I don't know how I sang so high. The maracas on that record were inspired by the Bell Notes song "I've Had It." We saw the band on TV, and the drummer played them. I loved that record. "Fight Fire" is a pretty cool little song. That's our best British Invasion imitation.

Sometimes we'd take a step back because our ambition was too grand, or maybe we went left a little bit, doing something off character, but it seemed like things were getting better and better as we moved along. The guys were learning their instruments a bit as we played more and more. And our songs—the ones we wrote and the covers we played our own way—were starting to sound like "us," getting closer to that thing where it sounds "right."

Now, I'm not saying the Golliwogs were very good—it was not a real band yet, commanding a stage. We were lightweight, thin. We were just kids. But hey, we'd gotten the hook opening for

Sonny and Cher! And it was a fun time. It was so innocent. We're not making it, we're not hitting the big time, but maybe, just maybe, we... *could.*

There were big changes in my life at this time. In 1965 I got married. I had met Martha Paiz while I was working at the gas station. She'd come in with her sister and her sister's boyfriend. I started talking to Martha that way. We were children when we got married. I was twenty years old. Martha proposed to me. I don't remember the exact words — "We should get married" or something like that. I had a typical male response: "Uhhh...okay."

There really ought to be a law. Probably one out of ten of those marriages is going to work. At eighteen, Tom had left home and married his high school sweetheart, so there was some precedent in my immediate family. I was also tossed out of my house by my mom — "Just go there!," meaning over to Martha's. She wanted to be done with raising a feisty boy.

My mom even declared that I had to pay rent if I wanted to stay at home. That's something Julie and I have vowed not to say to our kids. Both of our parents booted us out.

My mom and I had sort of an estranged relationship after that. I think she saw Creedence only once, in Oakland. (Although Mom was the one who told me that Chet Atkins played "Proud Mary" with the Boston Pops. I detected that she was proud of that — and so was I!)

Martha's family was very much a family. She had a whole bunch of brothers and sisters, a large family, and when I'd go over and hang at their house, it was a real warm and happy feeling. There was this sense of closeness, whereas my house had just been depressing. So that had a lot of appeal to me. I moved right out of my home and into married life.

And then I got drafted.

CHAPTER 6

Dirty Little Wars

IN 1966, VIETNAM was on every young person's mind. The draft loomed large. We'd start to talk about it and ask each other, "Well, why are we in Vietnam?" And we'd go around and around and around and never really have a good answer.

In the early stages of the conflict, I was more gung ho, thinking that's what America should do. But the reasoning started sounding more and more flimsy. Most of it was just a sham: a couple of egocentric politicians too full of themselves to listen to their own people, and who had the incredible arrogance to send our young kids off to die. My generation just thought it was the most sorry, useless exercise that our country could be involved in, and we were powerless to stop this stupid thing but trying our darnedest through protests, music, and all the rest.

At the time, I really didn't understand all the implications, but as I got older, I began to feel that the war (and probably most every war that's ever been fought) wasn't actually about the flag: it was about a very small group of rich, powerful people, usually men, who were able to bamboozle a nation to go to war for some myth that they had created. This gets shrouded in patriotism, but it basically comes down to money. Making a profit. Vietnam was surely about that.

Regrettably, it's become a familiar story: the powers that be prey on the patriotic feelings of our youth, young people who have very noble ideals and want to go out and do what they assume are good things. But in situations like this, they're just being manipulated. That's the part that really makes me mad—even now, because I believe that the wars we're in are not for the good of America or the American people. Just for some businessmen to make a lot of money.

To use American citizens—basically kids—to fight and die for big corporations so they can make billions of dollars is just shameful. And to present it as if it's some patriotic thing, when it's just because a gas company wants to monopolize the market in another part of the world, or some big steel company wants to build all the buildings and bridges there—to have people die for that?

But I wasn't thinking about this back before I was drafted. I wasn't even going to be drafted—I was classified 4-F, meaning unfit for service. That was a good thing. I know a lot of people would say, "God, how unpatriotic. You're supposed to go out and fight for Uncle Sam." I'm sure in some quarters there are folks who will have strong feelings about what I'm saying. It'll strike some as vaguely un-American, even cowardly. I get that. Now, had I been around in the wake of Pearl Harbor, I'm quite certain I would've felt differently. But Vietnam was something else. Most of us felt that if you got drafted, you were going to Vietnam. And if you went, you were probably going to die. It didn't feel like, "Oh, here's my chance to be a hero for my country!" Being drafted, you could just immediately see the other end of it. So I received my 4-F classification, and I was smiling.

A couple of months went by before they sent a letter saying,

"Oops! We made a mistake. You've been reclassified. You are 1-A." And after that I got my draft notice.

I lost my job at the gas station because I told the manager the news, and he still said, "John, you have to come into work today." I said, "Al, I just got drafted! In thirty days I'm gone! I have to go out and see if there's anything I can do." So I was fired.

I went out looking at the Army Reserve and National Guard in the Bay Area, but they were full and couldn't take any more people. I came home from one of those days a little distraught, and my wife, Martha, told me she had called a reserves unit. There must've been something in her voice talking to that sergeant down at the Army Reserve, because he told her, "You just tell him to come on down here." I told him my story and he signed me up. He must have put a certain date on my papers—perhaps a date that was earlier than when I received my draft notice—so that I had officially signed up *before* I got my notice. I was now in the Army Reserve. I never actually got to thank that guy again. He was an awesome, soulful person.

The first time I went on active duty was at a two-week summer boot camp. One sergeant in particular just liked the sound of my name. "Hey, *Fo-ger-ty!*" "Where's *Fogerty?*" I got...noticed. And I didn't like it. There could be a group of fifty guys standing there, and you'd hear, *"Hey Fogerty!"* It was horrible. I was called every time.

So when I went on my six-month active-duty boot camp, I had learned my lesson. Don't do anything where you're straggling behind, don't do anything where you're stepping out ahead—just be in the group. Man, be somewhere in the shadows. Try to be invisible. Once the sergeant snags your name, you're toast.

So that's what I did. I became a model of responsibility. Unlike many other times in my life where I had been a flake (such as playing hooky for weeks), I remade myself into the company man. They had all this stuff you have to do: have your bunk made the right way, have all your clothes exact, your uniform spotless. It's good training, good discipline. And I did it exactly right—all of it. I was on the A-list.

After a couple of weeks, I got assigned as a barracks leader and was put in charge of a row of bunks. The guy over us noticed that I was getting it done, and by putting me in charge, he had a lot less to do. So I would be after my guys: put your toothbrush away, your shoe-shining kit, your underwear. Everything had to be in a specific spot, and I made sure it was.

I'd have all my ducks in a row. I was terrified of being caught, frankly. I didn't want them to ever notice me again. Which I think was a good philosophy, but the other guys got to calling me Ma Fogerty. It was with some affection and respect, but they might as well have called me Old Man Fogerty. They thought I was acting like somebody's parent! But it kept us out of trouble. We were all twenty years old, kids, and liked rock and roll. There's that whole sense of, yes, you're in the military, but you're twenty, not fifty. But I didn't want to be snagged. Once you're on the shit list, you're not coming off. I learned my lesson the first time.

When I came back from active duty, I still had my once-a-month reserve meetings and, every summer, two-week boot camp obligations. All of that was going to last another four or five years. And I kept having conflicts. My monthly weekend meeting was in Richmond. I'd have to be there at 7 a.m. after doing a gig four hours north in Roseville the night before. I overslept a couple of times and the sergeant called me up: "You want me to send you to *Vietnam?*" That was the threat they held over you. I knew I couldn't let it happen again or they'd send me.

I very earnestly tried to work something out. I wanted to come in during the week and I wanted to have long hair. I was the quartermaster supply clerk, and I could've easily done my job during the week. And of course the answer came back, "*No,* we can't have any of *that.*" They were pretty rigid.

At certain times in my life I can get pretty tough mentally — it's just a matter of focusing, I guess. Once I really had the door slammed in my face by the army and realized that they weren't going to entertain some other approach, I decided that I was going to resist, go against the grain. And try to get myself removed from the reserve. But in the calmest way possible.

I started fasting. Like prisoners on strike or Buddha fasting under a fig tree. During this time, the Golliwogs played a show at the Claremont Hotel, and I was on my fast, hardly eating anything. I remember staring at a table of lemon meringue desserts, but no — I didn't take one. I had a brain of steel. This was a very volatile time in America, with all kinds of confrontation and conflicts and philosophies floating across the cultural windscreen. People chaining themselves to government buildings. If I had to chain myself to an army building, I was prepared.

I wrote honestly about my plight to my congressman, Jerome Waldie — yes, I brought it to Jerome — and he was pretty helpful. That carried a lot of weight. He started kicking tires around the Army Reserve unit. That got their attention. They don't like the people's representatives peeking in the window at all their shit.

I became skinny as a rail, and because of the stink I was raising, the army made me go to the Presidio in San Francisco for an evaluation. My friends in the band gave me herbs to imbibe, supposedly to calm me down and make me weird. I was not a big pot smoker, yet there I was, driving across the Bay Bridge, smoking a joint on my way to be evaluated by the army. All I can say is, it wasn't my idea and the Big Lebowski would have been proud.

I told the evaluator that I was very upset and didn't agree with the war. I didn't sleep very well. By now Martha and I had an infant son, and I had experienced a couple of dreams where I was literally stabbing babies with a bayonet. I told the evaluator I'd lost a lot of weight. He said, "Well, how's your libido?" I didn't know what that meant. I looked at him and said, "What's a libido?" I think the fact that I was that stupid—and that I didn't have a big, long, over-the-top scenario, wasn't really there with a prepared case—might've swayed the day a little in my favor.

I saw a lawyer. I remember writing to various causes, even the Black Panthers. I was trying anything I could think of. I even showed up at boot camp with a syringe. Just planted it in my stuff, waiting to be found. I might've got it from Martha's mom because she worked in nursing. It was new, unused, and I didn't have what went with it. It was more just to be scary—"What's *this*, Private Fogerty?" If they had actually said, "Okay, tell us what you do with that," I wouldn't have had a clue!

The head of our reserve unit was this guy, Lieutenant Ritzman. He was a second looey—typical military guy. I think Ritzman was in the reserves, just like me, but he took it way more seriously. A real brownnoser. We had this big meeting, almost like a social get-together, semicasual, and he's doing armyspeak. A pep talk. We're kids—he's late twenties, I'm barely twenty—and he starts by quoting *Laugh-In,* I guess to be hip. Then he says, "America has a counterculture and the army has to tread carefully. As you folks know, there's been a lot of demonstrations, protests. Civil disobedience. Unruly crowds. Where we will have to control the situation, not let it get out of hand. So when we arrive, we don't want to be doing our formations out in the open. We will go around to a side street..."

Slowly it's dawning on all of us that he's talking about using the U.S. Army (and perhaps our reserve unit) to keep protesters in line, keep people down. The idea was to get into formation, out of sight from the disturbance, and then come around the corner in full force as an organized show of military muscle. At the time, I think it was illegal to use the army for that. We have a National Guard for internal domestic emergencies. He kept talking like this for fifteen minutes.

Finally, I raised my hand and stood up. I'm feeling somewhat cynical and sarcastic. We've all seen pictures of Red Square. You know, the Soviet Union parading its military might around the Kremlin for all to see and be intimidated. So I said, "Why don't we just have the military parade all our rockets and tanks down the main street of every major city, y'know, like, once a month? Just show 'em the army's muscle, our might. I think that would keep people in their place." I sat down.

You could see the steam coming out of Ritzman's ears. After that, I showed up at my reserve meeting with my gray Peugeot 403 plastered with signs I had made. "Warning—the Army Is Coming!" "The Velvet Glove Is Off, the Iron Fist Is Revealed!" Well, they noticed.

"Susie Q" was already happening, and with the guys in tow, I took the same leaflets down Macdonald Avenue, the main street of Richmond, near where we lived, and started taping these things onto telephone poles and streetlights. We get about two blocks and a cop car pulls up. We get arrested and taken to the Richmond city jail. It's illegal to post signs on the light fixtures. The officer could barely contain himself. He was a patriot; we were long-haired hippie types. They held us there a few hours. I think our one phone call was to Al Bendich, the lawyer at Fantasy.

These activities started to weigh in my favor. Eventually I saw this guy, Mr. Legere, at the Presidio. He was on the army base and part of the military, yet he was a civilian. And Mr. Legere was a good guy. The first time I sat in his office and told him my tale, there was one thing he said that blew my mind: "Wow, it's rather like a story by Camus." I'd been in the army awhile and had never met anybody like that. I could sense that Mr. Legere was willing to help because I think he respected how I was going about it. I

wasn't a wacko. Even though I was against the war—I think he
was too—I was clearly just trying to support my family. He could
sense that I was trying to do right, trying to find a way to work
within the system.

This process went on for several months. I was never sure how
it would all turn out, but I kept trying everything I could think of.
Of course, I had to keep going to reserve meetings and treading
carefully through these treacherous waters. I believe I met with
Mr. Legere at least one more time at the Presidio, and we spoke by
phone several times throughout this ordeal.

It was starting to get near summertime, and they were going to
send me to camp again, this time to Camp Roberts. I was even
skinnier now. Mr. Legere seemed to think we were getting close to
a discharge for me, and we were feeling hopeful about that. But
one day he tells me, "I think it would be a good idea if you could
get a medical to avoid that camp this summer, because you know
what's going to happen if you go."

He was right, of course. There was going to be a great *big*
bull's-eye on my back—"There's that wimp that's trying to get
out of the reserve. Let's get him."

I went to my doctor at Kaiser Permanente. They needed to do
all these blood tests. I hate shots and having my blood taken, but I
sat there like a good soldier while they took vial after vial of my
blood. They needed to take thirteen vials, and I thought they were
done, but I had miscounted. Feeling a little woozy from losing
blood, I heard them say, "Oh no, we're not done—we need to
take *one* more..." I just sorta crumbled onto the tabletop and lost
consciousness. At that point, I think I weighed 129 pounds.

Turned out I had a mild form of dysentery. The report said, "If
you turn this guy loose in the camp, it's not so much what it's
gonna do to him, it's what he's gonna do to everybody else! You're
all gonna get sick. This thing will spread like wildfire." Thank
you, Mr. Legere. Sometime in midsummer of 1968 I received my

discharge, and as far as me being in the army, that was that. My army days were over.

There was a time when I could barely talk about Vietnam. Since I was lucky enough to get into the reserve, I wasn't sent to Vietnam. I wasn't in combat. There was such an anxiety in those years over whether or not I was ever really going to go. I managed not to. But I was and still feel very much a part of that generation, and the whole thing that was going on all around us. Yeah, maybe I looked like a hippie wacko, but as a guy in a rock and roll band who was exactly the same age as those soldiers, I tried to represent the cause as best I knew how. It would just bring me to my knees, it was so sad and very real to me. I must admit that practically every time I'd think about the guys, our vets, I would cry. I'd hear "Where Have All the Flowers Gone" on the radio and would lose it. Because it was just so senseless.

I know of so many people whose lives were ended or ruined, families that lost a kid. Let alone all the broken lives that came home—"Why is Daddy so fucked up?" People having flashbacks who can't talk about it, won't talk about it. All that carnage and fear. I know how I felt about Richard Nixon grinning at me through the damn TV screen like some kind of clown, calling the protesters at Kent State "bums." Where was Richard Nixon when our soldiers were out in a rice paddy? Those soldiers were pretty much just thrown out there on their own to improvise. Hopeless. I still feel sorrowful about those times.

I remember that day in 1974 when it came on the radio that we had ended the war in Vietnam—well, we were withdrawing. The thing we had been telling Nixon to do for five years: just *leave*. He didn't want to be the only president who had ever lost a war, so the damn fool had said to push on (just like in the song). Now it was finally over. I was driving in my jeep and had stopped at a light, and I can remember just shaking my head and going, "Let's just make damn sure we never do somethin' that stupid again." As I looked through the windshield, this thought formed: *Y'know, I still don't know what we were fighting for.* Down through the years, I've wanted to have that be the last line of a song: "And they've still never told me what we were fighting for."

The real answer is, we were fighting for businessmen, fighting for guys to get rich. Not for me, not for my friends out there in the field, but for the guys who own companies wrapped up in military contracts, the guys paving the roads, building the buildings, making the bridges, and finding the oil—all that crap. Those people who want your kid to die so they can get rich. And if you look at our kids today, that's still pretty much what they are fighting for.

The Vietnam generation is aging but has remained soulful. In the nineties I was helping with a benefit for the Berkeley Hall School. This is where all our kids went to school. It was a sweet little place, and Julie and I tried to support it in whatever way we could. They were having an auction, and she decided that something special I could contribute was some autographed handwritten lyrics. So I wrote out the words to "Bad Moon Rising" and signed them. I usually print, since my handwriting is horrible, plus my signature's a mess—I don't have the John Hancock gift. So I worried about it.

The event arrives and we attend. I wonder how my little contribution turned out, so I go to have a look. It's been framed, and I'm standing there reassuring myself: "Okay, John, it's not that bad." And I feel the presence of somebody beside me, someone I don't know. He looks at the lyrics and says, "You're John, right? That's your song, 'Bad Moon Rising'?"

"Yes, sir," I say.

He says, "Your song means a lot to me."

"Really?"

"Yes. Can I tell you a little story? I was in Vietnam."

Now he's really got my attention. Nice-looking guy, dressed well, looks good.

"I was in a little group. We called ourselves the Buffalo Soldiers. We had a little encampment, and every night our assignment was to go out into the jungle, find Charlie, and engage Charlie."

The wheels are spinning in my head now.

"So we called ourselves the Buffalo Soldiers to kind of brace ourselves up. We had a little PA system and lights. Every night, just before we'd go out into the jungle, we would turn on all the lights in our encampment, put on 'Bad Moon Rising,' and blast it as loud as we could."

I'm looking at him, thinking, this was crazy—suicide. "Why did you do that?"

"Because we were about to go into the jungle."

"And you're announcing it?"

"Yep. 'Here we come.' "

And I thought to myself, *How profoundly courageous and fatalistic*. They knew they were doomed. Whose crazy idea was this assignment? Sometimes all is lost and all you can do is be brave. No matter how you feel about it, there's no other choice. These guys were being brave to the nth degree.

"Anyway, John, I just want to thank you, because your song really helped a lot of us in what we had to do over there."

I shook his hand. I wish I could remember his name. He had done what was asked of him and didn't cry or whine about it, as opposed to me. He had done something I didn't do, something I'm not sure I could've ever done. And he certainly had my respect.

In his heart he has a connection with that song and me. And to hear from others like him that my music helped them in some way, helped GIs endure what they had to go through? You feel a little sheepish in the presence of something like that. I sure wasn't taking any bows.

I just looked at him and said, "I'm really glad you made it through."

You could say that one good thing happened to me in the army. It was 1967, and I went on duty right at the end of January and didn't get out until July, one day before I would've qualified for all the benefits that the government can give you—"Okay, let's get his butt outta here. Otherwise he's gonna get the GI plan."

They drafted millions of guys and didn't know what to do with us. They're trying to keep you busy from the time they wake you up at five thirty in the morning until you finally get off at seven at night. They're keeping you moving the whole time. So you're marching, marching, marching every day.

I was sent to Fort Bragg, Fort Knox, and Fort Lee. By the time I got to Fort Lee, summer was raging. They had this massive, mile-square parade field made out of asphalt. The heat coming off that black asphalt felt like an oven, and you've got on your army fatigues, boots, and rifle, and you just march, march, march. You could go for miles. It was endless.

I started to get delirious. In the military, you try to make the toes of your boots shine like glass. Black glass. Shiny like an expensive car. You could see yourself in them. Spit shined. As I'm marching along, I imagine that there's this one smudge. This stinkin' smudge. I go to shine it, and it keeps moving—"I'm over here!" I'm rubbing it, but it moves and won't go away. I'm a little crazy at this point: delirious, rubbing, rubbing, rubbing. And somehow this evolved into thinking about music.

I started thinking about a story—a character from the wrong side of the tracks, sort of a put-upon guy, whose dad was frowned upon in the community because he may have stolen something, committed some kind of crime. It was me, but it wasn't me. Not specifically my own life, but enough of me in there. It could've been a Tennessee Williams play.

I kept doing this, day after day. I'd kind of click on the station in my head, and the same story would start to play. It was comfortable...soothing. "Okay, I'm going there. Okay." March, march, march. Grunt, grunt, grunt. At some point I became self-aware. At first it was like you're swimming in a stream—your mind is so busy that you don't realize what you're doing. You're just trying to survive. "The army thinks they have me but they don't. They don't have *what's in my mind*."

I thought, *Man, you're onto something here. This is better than "Have you ever been lonely, have you ever been blue, boo, hoo, hoo,"* and all the teenage angst songs I had known. This was more meaty, it had some serious stuff in it, and it resonated with how I *felt*. And I realized, *I'm writing a song*. It was music. That song eventually became "Porterville."

I think more people listen to "Porterville" and identify with the guy who feels like he's on the wrong side of the tracks than with the mob that came and took his dad away to serve his time. They probably don't want to be the lawmen. They probably don't want to be the dad in the song. In other words, the character telling the story—he's the common man. A perspective. How I look at the world. Which runs pretty much throughout all the songs I write, or at least the good ones. Because "Porterville" really is how I look at the world, and have for a long time. That's where I'm comin' from, as people say. It isn't made up, it isn't a fairy tale, it's not fake. I might take poetic license describing a situation, but the personal truth, the truth of my station in life, is in there.

You'll notice I never say "Porterville" in the song. I wanted it to be a small town. I could've named it "Merced." Or "Turlock." I just wanted a certain feel to it and eventually found Porterville, and that sounded *exactly* right.

So this thing I did while I was marching in the army really became my first narrative song. Something was coming into my head—it was above me, it was above anything I had done before. It had a scene in it, a place that felt right to me, an emotion about why something is right or wrong. It was *about* something. I hadn't done anything like this before.

It's one thing the army did give me that will last a lifetime.

It was a new way of looking at a song.

CHAPTER 7

Susie Q

WHEN I CAME off active duty in the summer of 1967, the band had a different frame of mind. Before I went into the army, we weren't great, particularly with the timing issues—"What's a shuffle beat?" Before that, practicing was something we did to learn a new song or when we were getting ready to record. Now we were going to be more serious. We decided—all four of us— that we wanted to start getting good. So we made a regimen of practicing every day. This was maybe going to be our last fling at this big dream.

Doug and Stu had moved in together, kind of out in the country, in El Sobrante. They had rented a little house that was actually painted pink. And because of a certain book, they called it the Shire. I remember rehearsing "Good Golly, Miss Molly" there, and "Ninety-Nine and a Half (Won't Do)." And, of course, "Susie Q."*

Every day Tom and I would drive out together. We'd sit, drink

---

* Later we rehearsed in Tom's garage. The El Cerrito police showed up because we were so loud. Then we moved to a little shack behind the house, where Doug lived with his wife. I remember working on "Midnight Special" there. Eventually the cops showed up there too.

coffee for half an hour, and talk—most of it about music, a little about politics: Eugene McCarthy, the Vietnam War, Nixon. That was good, motivational.

And we'd talk about records we'd heard. One album that had come out while I was in the army was Albert King's *Born Under a Bad Sign*. Here was Booker T. and the MGs, my favorite band, backing this guy that I hadn't heard much about before. Albert was so awesome on that record, and the band played with such command. We all loved it. I bet that happened countless times— musicians my age taking note of *Born Under a Bad Sign*. Cream certainly did. We kind of adopted that as a high-water mark. Unbelievably enough, a little over one year later Albert King would be opening for us at the Fillmore.

We were deep into a pretty healthy time for the band. We were gung ho. Tom made a statement: "John is our leader. When John says, 'Jump,' we should say, 'How high?'" It was acknowledged that I seemed to have a clearer idea of what we should be doing musically, because not only was I able to sing, but I understood the music enough that I could teach. This was different from a bunch of guys showing up who could already play. It was clear that I knew how the instruments should sound. My arrangements of songs and my own playing and singing had become more focused too, and I was having more visions of the future. Because with everybody trying, I had the belief that we could actually achieve our dream. All this is happening within months, really.

In August, I started telling the band, "Something's gonna happen in October." Now, I had no clue. I didn't have any inside information. But the notion just kept coming to me and I kept saying it: "Something's gonna happen in October, and it's gonna change things."

And what happened was this: Saul Zaentz, along with some backers, bought Fantasy away from the Weiss brothers. Saul called us to a meeting at his house in early October 1967 and said,

"I have just purchased Fantasy Records, and I want to sign you guys." Saul seemed like our friend. He had been the sales manager at Fantasy. Whenever we would come in, we'd see Saul at his desk, and he struck us as less crazy than the others. He seemed to be our ally. Now Saul was going to be the guy in charge, and he wanted to give us a real shot.

So the first thing out of our mouths was, "Can we change our name?" And that is the way it happened, because there is no other way. I've read that Saul takes credit for that. We said it to him first, because we *hated* being Golliwogs.

So Saul said, "Yeah, of course."

We asked, "Can we finally go and make a real record in a real studio? Not in the lean-to?"

And he said, "Yeah, I think that'll be all right." Then he added, "I want us to have a new contract because I'm gonna be the new owner, and I don't want the Weiss brothers saying you're under contract to them."

We all looked at each other. We felt like we had been working a lot harder now. Our intent wasn't to keep doing it the way Max Weiss had done it. We wanted to change our name and make a living at this. We were all still poor as church mice. The idea of actually "making it" was such a faraway concept that nobody even knew what that would mean—but it might have meant getting a song on the radio. Or making enough money off a record to buy a new car. Y'know, like a hit group! Like the Beatles or something!

Doug Clifford said to Saul, "What if we make it, and we're successful?"

Saul said, "I will tear up that contract and we will get a new contract."

I'm sure Doug remembers that to this day, because it was kind of addressed to him. And us. That was Saul's response: we will tear the contract up. I think he added, "We all share equally in this thing." We felt that Saul was our partner. He was penniless, broke, driving a five-year-old station wagon, and operating Fantasy out of that car. So the way Saul explained it to us was that we were part of the business. We were not just that stupid group called the Golliwogs; we were now partners making this business go. That's how we all felt, this group of five people. All for one and one for all. We *were* Fantasy Records. There was not another living soul there. We were it.

Almost instantly, we started trying to think up a new name for the band. All I can say is that most of them were pretty dreadful. We'd sit around at these coffee sessions: "How about…?" I remember Stu called me up one day and suggested the name Hardwood. I think Doug came up with Gossamer Wump and Gumby.

Tom was the one who suggested the word "credence." Our friend Jerry lived in an apartment building where the custodian was named Credence Nuball. He was South African—it was his real name. So Tom suggested we name our band Credence Nuball and the Ruby. I thought of the name Whiskey Rebellion, and for, like, a minute I liked it. It had a kind of funky sound to me, obviously reflecting my love of history—especially American history. Also, I really liked the idea of our band having a renewal, a resurgence. Whiskey Revival? That wasn't any better than the rest. If some guy comes up and hands you a lug nut, it's up to you to say, "No, I'm not going to be a lug nut." I knew I'd know the right name when I heard it. So for almost three months we kept coming up with names and rejecting them.

Then, on Christmas Eve of 1967, I was watching TV and this commercial for Olympia Beer came on in glorious color. The image was this wonderful enchanted forest with a bubbling brook, everything green and mossy. Their motto was "It's the water." I'm pretty sure it was the Beach Boys singing beautifully in the background. The very next thing that came on was a black-and-white public service announcement for clean water. An antipollution commercial—a concept that was just starting to fly in America. It showed a stream full of cigarette butts and Styrofoam cups, and on the screen it said, "Write to CLEAN WATER," and it gave a Washington, DC, address.

Even though it plainly said "clean water," my mind turned it into "clear water." *Clearwater.* Wow...I liked that. It sounded kind of Native American. I had a great love for their lore and history, and for figures like Geronimo, Sitting Bull, Crazy Horse, and Chief Joseph.

Right there I went back to the word "revival." Clearwater Revival. That just wasn't quite...unique enough. This was all happening in a nanosecond.

Suddenly the word "Creedence" came to me. "Creedence" meant credibility, belief—it had a spiritual sound. "Clearwater" instantly had a *positive* vibe, a point of view, a sense of history, culture, Americana. My mind was racing, a million thoughts at once. Somehow the words "Creedence" and "Revival" were swirling around in this tumbling torrent of thoughts. I'm not sure in which order the words were first connected, but I do remember that I had to juggle them around a bit. Was it Clearwater Creedence or Clearwater Revival? This was all happening in a matter of a few seconds, maybe a minute or two. Suddenly it just popped: Creedence Clearwater Revival. I *loved* it. But I thought, *Wow, that's a mouthful.* It sounded even more American. It told you this was an American rock and roll band, and it was unique. So that's how it all kind of clanged together in my head.

Then I had to sell it. I knew the personalities in my band well enough to know that I had to not take ownership of the name. It had to look like it was in the air and just happened. The other guys were not all that sure. I'd write it out—"See how that looks?" I think Tom might've convinced them. No more Golliwogs. We were now Creedence Clearwater Revival.

I remember telling the guys at the time, "The name is better than we are." We were a Top 40 band playing clubs. Playing more distinctly than we had a year ago, but still kind of messy. Not organized, not powerful.

But by February I had come up with the idea of recording "Susie Q."

In January 1968, we signed the new contract with Fantasy Records that Saul Zaentz had requested. Sometime after that October meeting at Saul's house, he gave me the contract and I took it back to the band. We had agreed that in Creedence every band decision had to be a unanimous one. If one person said no, the matter was vetoed.

Now, I wasn't the most sophisticated guy in the world, and I knew that I could read that contract until the end of time and not know what it meant. We didn't have any legal representation—it was just us four guys. Stu was a business major, and his dad, Herman, was a prominent Bay Area attorney. So we all decided to give the contract to Stu so Herm could look it over.

One thing I've learned over the years is that when you are trying to make a deal with another entity, there is back and forth dialogue over the contract. You negotiate—it's expected. They propose something; you send it back with a counteroffer. The lawyers haggle, hopefully with input from you, and an agreement is eventually reached. I didn't know that then, but a prestigious attorney like Herman Cook certainly would have. That's the very reason we asked Stu to take the contract to him. So that should've been done for us. It wasn't. We were too dumb to know anything about that—all of us. I mention this because in the years since, Stu has been in the press talking about what a terrible businessman I was, and how I messed it all up for the group—*Boy, did John ef up.* Ironically, it was business major Stu who was supposed to get input from his lawyer father. Herm's only supposed advice was that it was okay to sign—no additions, no revisions, nothing.

Over the years, I have often wondered if Stu even showed the contract to his father.

About two weeks later, the band was at the Shire, loading up equipment for a show that night, and we were passing each other, carrying guitars, amplifiers, and drums. I remember this scene vividly, as I have replayed it many times in my mind.

One of us said, "Hey, Stu!"

Stu said, "Yeah?"

"What did your dad say?"

"What did Dad say about what?"

"What did your dad say about the contract?"

There was a pause. "He said, 'It's okay.'"

"Okay what?"

"It's okay to sign."

"Yay!" we all cheered. We were very happy.

Now, I certainly take responsibility—at least a quarter share!—for signing that contract on January 5, 1968. I've never said, "I was drunk!" Or "They pumped me full of morphine!" At the time, we thought Saul was our friend. He wasn't going to screw us, right?

But this contract would become infamous. And it would have a much more devastating impact on my life than it did for the rest of the band. Yes, it was terrible for all of us financially—our royalty rate (paid out of net sales, not gross) was 10 percent, increasing gradually to 12 percent over a few years—but for the creator of the material, there were long-reaching implications. Saul owned the copyright on all our songs, lock, stock, and barrel.

Fantasy was also now owed a number of songs per year, and if we didn't record them, the obligation would carry over to the next year. And the next. The grand total (which was actually upped in our second, June 1969, contract) amounted to 180 songs over seven years—and if not completed once that period ended, they'd *still* be owed. In 1969, Creedence's best year, we recorded three hit albums, but that only amounted to twenty-six songs. Besides me, nobody wrote songs in Creedence that amounted to anything, so when we broke up, the other guys were all set free. Not me. Fantasy Records had not only chiseled me out of a fortune, they still owned my future. I was enslaved.

That was all in the dark future, though. Right now we were four guys in a room with a dream. And Saul was in the same boat. How innocent it all was.*

I didn't hang out in San Francisco a lot—maybe went over to Golden Gate Park occasionally, headed to the Fillmore to see a few shows. But when I got off of active duty with the army, it was the Summer of Love, 1967. And there was a lot of attention being given to San Francisco culturally, musically, politically. I liked the politics. Because that's the way Pete Seeger talked: Be responsible for yourself and help your fellow man. Don't be a burden. Live and let live. Don't try to control everybody. I still feel that's the best way.

I always felt that I had everything in common with the other bands that way, and I liked that bands rather than record companies seemed to be controlling the thing. And the San Francisco scene seemed to be outside the regular music business. It definitely wasn't Los Angeles.

I felt connected with the San Francisco scene, but there were times when we'd see something there that would always bring home how different Creedence was. We went as a band to see Otis Redding at the Fillmore. To me he was so much better than almost anything else you could see there. Otis commanded that stage.

---

* Back in the nineties someone wrote a book about Creedence. I've always thought it was wack, even though I've never read it. How good could it be if the guy wrote a book about Creedence but never *talked* to me?

On the other hand, I remember going to Winterland—I can't remember if it was to see Jefferson Airplane or the Grateful Dead. Everybody was stoned. Somebody started to play and went into a guitar solo, and that was the whole set. Forty-five minutes of guitar solo. I was so frickin' out of there.

I reacted against that. What I had learned from James Brown and Jackie Wilson was how to *entertain*. When you're performing, it's a presentation. Watching Hank Ballard at the Oakland Auditorium, there was so much energy. There was competition, each act trying to outdo the other. The way the Grateful Dead and bands like that performed just seemed so sleepy. "And now, from San Francisco, the Grateful Dead!" They'd come shuffling out and everybody went to their amps—*bring, bwang, bwing.* They'd *tune up* for ten minutes. What?! Don't let them announce you until you're ready! "And now...*again*...the Grateful Dead!" When the Dead would jam, it seemed like they'd go off the path right away—and then *stay* off the path. Either you like that or you don't. In my world, I couldn't have my music be as unstructured as that. It makes me uncomfortable. They'd announce Creedence, and we'd tear out there, plug in, and *go!*

I think what I took most umbrage with was the stoned part, and that made me different from many of the San Francisco musicians. You dare not be stoned playing music around me. Not in *my* band. No. I talked about it then and I'll talk about it now. How are you going to do your best work stoned? Look, it's not that I'm anti-pot, especially in those days. It's a recreational deal. But when you're working, you're supposed to be working. I didn't want to see a drunk Dean Martin up there singing sloppy ballads either. Potheads always thought they were superior to the alcoholics. For one thing, they'd have a picture of a marijuana plant on their wall. My dad never had a picture of a Budweiser can on the wall. I sure as shit didn't want to see that. This was just an unhappy addiction to me.

Timothy Leary? What a jerk. A buffoon. I thought what he was doing was damaging. Lots of kids did stuff and probably hurt themselves because some official-looking guy like Leary told them it was okay. You'd be backstage at the Carousel Ballroom, and there'd be some guy who hadn't taken a bath in ages handing out greens or yellows or blues—yeah, it's free, but it might be arsenic. I didn't want any part of that, whatever it was. People were walking around with mystery pills. This scared me. LSD? I didn't want to jump out a window.

I could probably count on one hand how many times I smoked marijuana in my whole career. Okay, I'm exaggerating, but not by much. In the early days of Creedence, I remember sitting around the Shire stoned, and we were going to solve all the problems of the world...

As I mentioned, we had begun to practice every day, and we talked a lot about being more serious. There were many pot-smoking sessions at night where we discussed things like writing songs and being better on our instruments.

At one point we even adopted a pseudonym, "T. Spicebush Swallowtail," which was going to represent the songwriter on the tunes we would all write together. About this time, I went and got my little songwriting notebook. And I began to write songs, titles, ideas, etc. There was a lot of talking and a lot of pot smoking...a lot of being stoned and talking about doing this or that. This probably went on for a few weeks.

Every day we would meet at the Shire to practice. We would jam a bit and, after some time had passed, I would ask, "Does anybody have anything, any new songs?" And there'd be a silence and some mumbling. There is a quote from Ernest Hemingway about working on Hollywood movie projects that resonates with me. To paraphrase: "After all the talking, sooner or later someone is going to have to get down to the business of writing." So I would show the band what I had come up with on my own.

Things went on like this for a time, until it evolved into me just showing the band some songs and musical ideas. After a while I stopped asking if anybody had anything.

But the subject really remained open. It was not as if I had said, "Okay, you guys can't write any songs. I will write *all* the songs from now on." I simply got very busy and worked feverishly to come up with music for the band. I really did *not* want to go back to being an obscure band. If at any time the other guys had come up with a great song, I'm sure we would've jumped on it. But instead of actually doing the work, they contented themselves with grumbling about it . . . from the sidelines.

This is something that really ticks me off, in showbiz and in life. You know, people who complain about how they should have gotten this break or that part. . . . "They" stole my idea. . . . I coulda been a contendah. But these same people never do the work, never come up with anything of substance. We ended up using T. Spice-bush Swallowtail for only one single: "Porterville" / "Call It Pretending." I wrote both songs—by myself.

So there we were at the Shire, stoned, and we were gonna solve all the problems of the world. And the next day everything went right back to where it had been before. I guess we're not all gonna write "Strawberry Fields Forever." At some point the drugs wear off.

I don't mean to be on a soapbox or sound preachy. I wasn't a prude, and I didn't think I was above it—I just thought, *man,* be yourself while you're trying to make a record or perform in front of people. They want to see you at your best. I always viewed a live performance as kind of like a prizefight. Meaning you have to be in shape for this, give the most that you can to your fans.

I never wanted to feel that I let one get away from me, to have a show where I'd just gone out and been sloppy and awful and stupid. In the Jackie Wilson era, there seemed to be a sense of honor, a sense of duty, like, "I'm lucky to have this job. You should take it seriously, or pretty soon they're not going to let you *do* that job." I still feel that way.

I was always making this speech to the band. I had to be the general and I wanted us to rock. I didn't appreciate hearing, "Maybe it would be better if we're stoned." I think there were some instances later when the guys in the band tried to put one over on me because I was such a square. They tricked me a couple of times and did it anyway. And then blamed it on the Grateful Dead: "They put LSD in the coffee!" (Hell, you can blame *anything* on the Dead.) I thought we were better than that. I'm not going to say "smarter"; I'm going to say "better." Meaning that we were a band, and that for us, music was the most important thing.

What many British groups—even some American ones—had done when they first started out was show the world how well they played classic rock and roll. The Stones had "Not Fade Away," "Around and Around," and "Carol"; the Beatles did "Money," "Kansas City," and "Twist and Shout." They had their feet planted firmly in the tradition of rock and roll. With that in mind, I liked the idea of doing an old song instead of trying to come up with a new one. The point in my mind was not to worry about writing a new song, because we'd done that and it wasn't working. I said, "I'm gonna take a song I already know is a good song." And so I settled on "Susie Q."

We were all listening to KMPX, the cool underground FM station. It was counterculture, really outside the mainstream, but more and more people were gravitating toward it. Tom Donahue was the main deejay. They played the Dead, Jefferson Airplane, Quicksilver—all the happening San Francisco bands, but we'd also noticed that these guys were playing some songs that weren't actual released records. Unreleased tapes like Janis Joplin's "Hesitation Blues," and I think a tape by Kaleidoscope. There were a few of them. The deejays would play them and talk about them—on KMPX, that was as valid as hearing "Mustang Sally" or "Nights in White Satin." Instead of doing a whole album and going through a record company—I think we still weren't so sure about Fantasy Records anyway, and whether we'd ever break out of that recording shack—covering a classic song seemed like the quickest way to go.

I loved the 1958 Dale Hawkins record "Susie Q." Tom did too. I remember hearing it in my mom's car and just bangin' away on the dashboard. It has a great riff. *Great.* You'll notice that James Burton's name is not among the names of the people credited with writing "Susie Q." That's a crime. At least half of the song is that lick. It was somewhere during the Monkey Inn period that I sat down and said, "Y'know, I have to actually learn how this really goes. What's James doin' here?" His unique hybrid guitar picking was far ahead of its time, especially ahead of the Telecaster country pickers. James used a flat pick plus one metal finger pick. It gave "Susie Q" an edge. I thought, *I gotta figure out a way I can do that, but still use my regular flat pick so I don't have to change anything. I'm not Elmore James or Grandpa Jones—I'm a rock and roll guy.* I came up with a way of using two fingers and a pick. It was a cool thing. Nowadays they call it hybrid picking.

I'd been playing that song forever—with the Blue Velvets and at the Monkey Inn. We'd do the song every once in a while, and once we did it at some club, we'd play it for a couple of nights, and then stop. We were playing up somewhere in the Sacramento area in the beginning of 1968. Some club, people just milling about, and we could experiment and no one would care. I'm thinking about "Susie Q," and I turn to Doug and say, "Let's try somethin' a little different." I wanted it to have a gospel feel, but I didn't dare say to him "shuffle beat."

I said, "Try to get this feel: *doom chick, doom doom chick*." Doug starts imitating that. I go, "Right," and start playing the "Susie Q" riff. But I say, "Let's don't change—let's jam. We're not gonna play the song. Just stay in E." Stu's going, "Well, what should I play?" "Just stay in E, no pattern." That was the start of it. It was by no means what it became, but it was the format. At that time you had British Invasion, psychedelic music, folk rock. "Susie Q" stood out as a gutbucket, country blues thing. And people liked it.

"Susie Q" is a pretty simple song. After *Sgt. Pepper,* rock and roll grew up and everybody got all brainy and highfalutin and introspective and impotent—I mean important. Some people looked down on what made rock and roll what it is in the first place: fun. Loud, in-your-face, rebellious. Full of attitude. Definitely not "I have a dissertation that I must explain." I'm a guy who admires "Wooly Bully" as much as "The Times They Are a-Changin'."

We spent weeks preparing for the recording. We rehearsed the song out at the Shire, making it longer and longer in the solos. I remember saying to the other guys that it sometimes felt like I had an out-of-body experience playing "Susie Q." I'd actually forget where I was. When the song was over, I'd look around and realize, "Oh." And then we'd look at each other and play it again. There was a lot of playing that basic song as a four-piece band. But I was also making them settle down, instead of just jamming like at the Monkey Inn.

There were no defined musical parts yet. That was my job, because I could see what was missing. Clear as a bell. From "Susie Q" on, I realized that my job was to arrange everything, period. I'd been doing it somewhat before, arranging Golliwogs singles to sound vaguely like the Beatles, the Stones—and they did. With "Susie Q," I was going into new territory.

I had seen an old movie on the late show, *The Glenn Miller Story.* Miller's band has been struggling to find their identity, and they're rehearsing a make-it-or-break-it gig. The trumpet player busts his lip on his music stand, and all is lost. Miller stays up all night rewriting the lead for clarinet, and it changes the music. Everything falls into place— "That's the sound!" Having the right individual parts blended together. This made a big impression on me, and that's how I approached arranging.

In the sixties, everyone thought rock was free-form noodling. But look at the Beatles. Or more so the Ventures—it's even more obvious with them because their records are so bare. It's textbook how to play rock and roll. Listen to those records: it's very clear what each guy's role is. With the Ventures, you have a lead guitar, a rhythm guitar, a bass, and a drummer—there's not even a singer. Everything is planned out to sound a certain way together. Everybody is playing arranged, specific parts.

The idea of jamming was cool to me—challenging—but the point was that it had to be great, not one-note meandering, and none of that nobody-knows-what's-gonna-happen-next philosophy. I could not let that happen in my band. Be it "Susie Q," "I Heard It Through the Grapevine," "Commotion," or "Keep On Chooglin'," there was a structure. It was organized. There were parameters for how far out the song could go. I had to know darn sure what was going to happen, because I didn't want people falling asleep—the audience or the band. The difference between our jams and, say, the Dead's? In my band, there was an *arrangement*.

I'd tell the band, "Just try stuff. It's okay. When it's good, I'll smile." All through Creedence it was me either smiling yes or saying no. Even if they didn't know the parameters, I did, and if they got outside that, I would let them know. I always tried to explain why. I didn't just mysteriously say, "Here's your notes. Play them." Really, it was a friendly thing. But what you hear on the records is what I controlled.

I'd say, "When doing the drum fill, Doug, it should be this type, this style." I'd be right there working on a backbeat. Each instrument had a role to play, so the rhythm guitar had to be in a specific place, the bass in another. Or I'd be thinking to myself, *What's the bass part gonna be? I know it's gotta be* that *feel*. I would literally do it on the guitar, or in my mind. As Stu was playing it, I'd go, "No, no, no—lose that note." Whatever bass part the Dale Hawkins band was playing on the original "Susie Q" had to be changed to fit KMPX, a place where they played the Dead.

That was how I approached the jams. If we were learning a two and a half minute single, frankly, it was, "Here's how it goes and this is what you play." In Creedence, the learning curve was there each and every new song. By the time "Susie Q" was recorded, we would play it live, and it sounded pretty good. Then I'd start to show them a brand-new song, like "Born on the Bayou," and we'd sound like amateurs again! I'm not saying that as any kind of slam. It was just a weird phenomenon: the stuff we did out on tour was manly, authoritative, and then we'd go in to learn a new song, and it sounded like the Mickey Mouse Club.

Most of the time, when I rehearsed the band I didn't sing. I'd work out all the music ahead of time and then teach it to the band as an instrumental. It had to have a musical hook without any singing. And the guys learned the song without hearing me sing it. Because I didn't want to sing in front of them. I was a little shy about that. I still get a little funny when I'm going to show my band a song, even now. But *especially* then.

On the music side, I developed a formula: I would choose two songs for the singles and we would rehearse those two for six weeks. Of course, those six weeks started with just a snippet of a rhythm idea, trying many variations of chord structure and drum patterns. In this way, I could test-drive many different approaches of presenting the song until I felt I had arrived at the absolute best arrangement. There were dozens of little musical intersections along the way where you had to make a choice about which beat or note was best for that particular song. That's how you refine an arrangement and make it great. That is also how you get the musicians used to performing the music, so that after six weeks they are playing the thing like it's second nature.

Along the way, we'd work on the album cuts. So when we went into the studio to do "Up Around the Bend," "Run Through the Jungle," all the singles, take one would be awesome. It was, "Well, all right—maybe we can beat that." And certainly take three was about it. That was all you needed. Done! There was no point in doing any more. We had rehearsed it and we were ready.

I've heard Stu take credit for making "Susie Q" a "psychedelic" jam. No way. In spite of what Stu says, it is *not* a psychedelic jam. That recording was all planned out on paper. I did it by myself on the kitchen table. I don't know how to read music, so I sat down and taped pieces of binder paper together with Scotch tape because no one piece of paper was long enough, and I made a road map of the song showing what would happen *here,* and *here,* and *here*… all the way through. I turned music into pictures—that's how I took "Susie Q" from here…to there. It was, "I'm gonna take a journey with this song."

To me, a record is a presentation. It is not cinema verité, and all that other artsy crap that people were doing in the early seventies. No: a recording is a presentation. You've thought all about it, the arrangement, the mix—that's why you can hear the singer a little louder than the drum or the bass. You've *prepared* this. You need to have the music be a bed for your song, so it can *present* your song. One of the huge secrets of Creedence was that this music was brain-numbingly simple, but it's the *right* simple. I always said, "There's only one right way."

I feel like I was given the gift of having a very clear understanding of what to do. That might've been the greatest gift of all. You have to have a leader, and in that band, as in all bands, you need a purveyor of taste. If I was not the sole judge, I was certainly the final judge—"Now it's ready." Then we went and recorded it.

Call me a perfectionist? Guilty. I haven't been as anal about that process since Creedence—where I had that level of intensity with an arrangement and kept developing it before we recorded. "Susie Q" was the first time we ever worked on something that way. And that was the way it stayed—until the mutiny at the end of 1970.

We didn't record "Susie Q" in Fantasy's lean-to—I took us back to Coast Recorders and Walt Payne, the same guy who had engineered James Powell's "Beverly Angel" when I was fourteen. After we set up, it was our practice to jam and get comfortable, play some blues. Then we counted off "Susie Q" and recorded it—first take, *boom*. There was no take two. I had to go back another day and sing the vocal. When I got there, Walt said, "Well, Bing Crosby was here this morning singing through that mic, so I figured that would probably be all right for you." My mom loved Bing, and so did I. "Wow—*yessir!*" In the mix, part of my vocal was put through this thing that Walt called "the telephone box," which they would use on radio dramas when someone called on the phone.

There's a lot of little tricks going on in "Susie Q." I knew the song would start with the drums fading in. I tried other things. If you listen to the rhythm, there's something going *shhhhusha shusha*—that's me. It turned out Doug really couldn't keep that beat going on the sand blocks, so I played them. It's a big addition to the groove. It's a pretty cool beat, almost that sand and Vaseline thing. There's some backwards guitars, some tambourine backbeat, and an open piano where I held down the sustain pedal, dissonant notes, sort of a disturbing ambient sound but nestled pretty far back in the track. And the backing vocals—"fine"/"mine," "moon"/"June." We sat in a circle with a mic dropped between us, and I would strum a chord really quietly and we'd go "fiiiiiiiiiine...

miiiiiiiiine." We did that all by itself and then I inserted it into the mix. I knew what I wanted to do with it. I was kind of poking fun at Tin Pan Alley, how they'd use all these simple words that rhymed.

I distinctly remember being in the studio with the whole band the day we were preparing all the tracks for "Susie Q." They were sitting in front of the console down below, where the window out to the studio is. I've got this thing that I've mapped out. I've worked on this for weeks—it's my baby. I'm putting the different pieces together, the "fine/mine/moon/June" stuff, and I hear Stu: "That'll never work!" I was getting more and more annoyed. Some guys never recover from negativity like that. They're not strong enough to go, "Y'know what? Screw you!" I was trying to mix this. I knew what I was doing—I had a map! Even though my actions may have looked selfish at times, I was doing this for my band, what I thought presented us in the best way possible. My heart was in Creedence, and it stayed that way for a long, long, long time. Trying to be protective of the band, sometimes maybe in spite of itself. After "Susie Q," I never allowed them to be in the studio again when I was mixing. I didn't need that distraction.

People told me later that "Susie Q" was cool because it had so much guitar. I had another guitar and amp by then. While I was away in the army, Tom had taken my Mustang and maybe my Supro and traded them in. Those two were worth one short-scale Rickenbacker 325. That's the kind John Lennon played, and there seemed to be a trend in getting that kind of acoustic-electric sound. I also had a new Kustom K200 amp. Saul advanced the money for that: $1,200. We'd asked for money to get an old van and an amp. He would only give us money for the amp. Of course, I ended up paying for that amp out of royalties.

The Kustom was solid-state, with transistors. Everybody pre-fers tube amps, including me. I learned to pull everything I could out of that Kustom. God, I got a great sound out of that amp. "Susie Q" was practically a demo of what that amp could do. It has to be the right guitar with that amp. The Kustom was really, really loud, and it had a great, clean guitar sound—you can hear that on "Bad Moon Rising." Not *perfectly* clean, the way other transistor amps were—there's a little bit of grit, warmth—but it's not out of control. That amp had the killer vibrato of all time— listen to "Born on the Bayou," which came a bit later.

At Coast, they had one knob that we could pan from left to right. I remember Walt explaining that to me during the mixing of "Susie Q," and I thought that was the coolest thing. It's sort of irritating for me now, the way the drums are and how one guitar's way over here and the other guitar's way over there. Everything is on the left or the right; nothing sits in the middle. It's not real stereo.

I didn't know what stereo was then. I had never heard it. I didn't have a stereo radio, didn't have any stereo records, didn't have a stereo player. Then I got to Wally Heider Studios, and they had all kinds of knobs! Like, eight of 'em! I found out why. "Oh...they call that stereo."

When I was working with the guys on "Susie Q," one of them actually said, "Well, John's got an eight-track recorder built into his head." I already seemed very familiar with the whole recording situation. It was a compliment, but they were also talking about something they didn't have.

Despite all that, with "Susie Q" I really felt that we had hit the mark. I remember coming back after that session to play it for Saul in the old Fantasy offices on Treat Avenue. I said, "That's great." Saul goes, "Well...it's very good." I said, "No—that's *great*." In my heart, I knew that we had transcended to another level. The other song we recorded at that first session was Bo Diddley's "Before You Accuse Me," and the arrangement was not great. I call that the Jefferson Airplane version because it was kind of like "Somebody to Love." After it was done, I thought to myself, *Nah, I'd rather do it more like Bo's version. Who needs this?* We later rerecorded it. (That first version actually stayed undiscovered until Fantasy decided they wanted to put out every-thing, down to me picking my nose.)

I knew that "Susie Q" was it, and when we took the tape to KMPX, they loved it. They started playing it a lot. I would hear it at least three or four times every day. Awesome. We split the song into two parts for the actual single, and it became a Top 40 radio hit. I think we all knew this was really it.

A funny thing happened. We played a week at a place called Mousy's, in Davis, typical small college-town bar. "Susie Q" was new, still just a tape and not on the radio in Davis. We were jam-ming on it. I thought we'd played a pretty good version—we were really getting into it. As we neared the big finish, some guy from the audience laid a piece of paper at Tom's feet. It said, "Hey, you hippies—you're trying too hard!" Like, "That's not a normal song. You played the guitar too long. Knock it off!" We all got a big chuckle out of that.

Creedence had gotten a steady gig in San Francisco at a club called Dino and Carlo's—another residency like the Monkey Inn, but with an older, more professional crowd. One thing that happened there I'll never forget. At the time, I was broke, living with a wife and baby on literally twenty dollars a week. That was my allow-ance from Tom. We trusted him to dispense the money: he was the older person with a job. The rest came from whatever few dollars we got from playing somewhere. We managed one credit card, which we always maxed out. It was a kind of socialism—we had this much money, and each of us got what he needed. I got twenty bucks a week, which covered food and diapers. Plus I smoked Kools with filters. One time I walked into a Safeway and looked longingly at a newspaper and a candy bar. I remember thinking that the mark of a successful career would be, "I can afford a Hershey bar."

There weren't a lot of groceries at home. Late one night, I found a can of kidney beans and put them in a saucepan. The aroma woke Martha up. I was caught sneaking beans! I felt like the guy on the lost ship who's secretly hoarding all the food.

One night at Dino and Carlo's we were loading our equipment in, and some guy, a fan, reached out his hand and it's got twenty dollars in it. Well, you might as well have given me a cool million. I asked, "Should I split it with the band?"

He said, "Swing with it."

"You wanna hear a certain song?"

"No—swing with it."

The rest of the guys let me keep it. It was such an act of generosity. I might as well have won the lottery!

Another night, Saul came by and watched a couple of sets. We were doing "Susie Q," "Ninety-Nine and a Half (Won't Do)," "I Put a Spell on You," "Good Golly, Miss Molly," and "Hi-Heel Sneakers," most of which ended up on the first record. Saul said, "I think there's enough there that you can make an album." That was a step forward. Besides "Susie Q," we had already recorded "Porterville," which had come out as the first single under Creedence's name on Fantasy's subsidiary label Scorpio, because Saul hadn't quite taken over yet.* "Porterville" is very reflective of mid-sixties rock, British influence, psychedelic—stretching out, playing a little long. That guitar sound is like the Airplane on *Surrealistic Pillow,* although I didn't have any good equipment. Clean with a bunch of echo on it. I'm pretty sure we took that single to KMPX too. I don't know how often they played it, if ever. The flip side, "Call It Pretending," I considered pop in our old style, so I didn't even put it on the album.

We'd been doing "I Put a Spell on You" live, but not for long— I might've done it at the Monkey Inn. I loved the song, and loved

---

* "Porterville" had actually come out as a Golliwogs single. After we became Creedence it was rereleased.

Screamin' Jay Hawkins's whole thing. It was so out there and all by itself—*"MYUHAHAHAHA!"* Back in the fifties, he'd get wheeled out in a coffin and it would take him forever to open it and jump out. I've got to do something like that! Do they have plaid burial clothes?

That sustained drone solo in Creedence's version of "I Put a Spell on You"—that's the Rickenbacker and the Kustom. The weird sounds you hear at the beginning were done later in the mix. Those are my son Josh's baby toys. We had a jack-in-the-box, some pull toys, and one of those tops that hummed once it started spinning—*whoosh whoosh whoosh hummmm.* We recorded them, and then played them back at different speeds. The song fades out with that. It sounds like a spaceship—it's supposed to be the other dimension. On my five-cent budget, I was trying to come up with things that were cool, and it worked. We did all the overdubs at my other old haunt, Sierra Sound. Tambourines and maracas— that's what I remember.

On "Gloomy," I wanted something ominous, so we took boxes with gravel inside and marched on it like soldiers. That didn't turn out to be as cool as I'd hoped.

Saul actually asked to put his name on the first album as producer—"I want people to know that Fantasy is under new management." After that I made darn sure I got credit: "Arranged and produced by John Fogerty." I'd gotten that from Chet Atkins records, which is funny because many of his productions are just Chet and a guitar (but sound as full as any record with two hundred musicians). I liked the phrase "Arranged and produced by" because it was the absolute truth.

That first album—*Creedence Clearwater Revival*—came out on May 28, 1968. My first album on my twenty-third birthday. I've seen other dates listed, but sorry, Charlie: they got it wrong. I remember because I was on the radio with deejay Tony Pig, playing the album for the whole world. The liner notes were written by Ralph J. Gleason—that's where he says, "Creedence Clearwater Revival is an excellent example of the Third Generation of San Francisco bands." Meaning we weren't quite as good as the Grateful Dead or Quicksilver Messenger Service. If you look at the cover of our fifth album, *Cosmo's Factory*—which is a shot of the band hanging out in the rehearsal space–office we called the Factory— you'll see a handwritten sign pinned to the top of one of the posts in the room: "3RD GENERATION." That was for Ralph.

As I mentioned, we had decided that everything in the band had to be voted on, and it had to be a unanimous decision. If one guy said no to whatever was being decided, then that was it: we didn't do it. And if something was voted on and came to pass, it stayed that way. It didn't change later unless we voted unanimously to change it. This is the way Creedence operated, and continued to operate for years and years, even after we broke up.

We also agreed that if the group ever broke up, we wouldn't allow one or two of us to run off and call ourselves Creedence Clearwater Revival. We had seen other groups do this over the years, like the Platters or the Diamonds, where some fraudulent version would be out there with one or maybe none of the original members. We agreed that either we were all in the band or else it just couldn't be.

And I gave the other guys equal share in the songwriting income. As I've mentioned, for a very short time the band used a pseudonym that referred to all four of us as a songwriting entity: T. Spicebush Swallowtail. (Doug knew a little bit about the world of entomology, and a spicebush swallowtail is a species of butterfly.) It's used on both sides of the "Porterville" single. In the all-for-one spirit of Creedence, we were going to use that for all the songwriting credits. Early on, we didn't know that I'd be the guy writing all the songs—but now that the first album was done (and

I was already writing songs for our next album), I began to realize that the credit wasn't fair. It was a matter of pride. I felt that if I had written the song, it should have my name on it.

Now, I didn't want to keep changing the agreement the way the white man did with the Indians, so what I said was, "I will share all the songwriting money equally until the end of 1969." So the guys got royalties for songs they did not write, on four albums that each sold well over a million copies by the end of 1969.

I did that so the other guys would not feel anxious about the money. I was sharing, being generous, because this was my band. The only thing I was counting on was this agreement of unanimity in the group. We were blood brothers, and we gave our word. That's still the law to me.

Creedence was starting to make a stir. You could see we were comers. But we weren't there yet.

Just as the first album came out, we played this weird pizza place near the Stanford University campus. It was a college hang, a daytime gig, small potatoes. We're setting up and I overhear two guys in the audience talking. I was dressed very casual for this gig, and this guy sees my white canvas sneakers and says to the other one, "Oh man—I thought these were, like, *cool* guys." Meaning my wardrobe sucked, and this was a great big hole in his vision of the band. Instead of being crushed or remaining oblivious, I knew exactly what he was talking about. You want to see what you hear. When I first heard the Animals, I said, "We've had the Beatles, we've had the Stones. The *Animals,* man: what are they gonna look like?" I figured it would be guys in loincloths and bones going, *"Aaarrrrh!"* They were the *Animals.* Then they come out and they all had these neat little suits on. It was a bit underwhelming.

So this guy staring at my sneakers was absolutely right. That changed immediately. I never wore those to a show again. Because how I look ought to go with how I sound: cowboy boots, Levi's, plaid shirts. Basically, my vision of myself. Image is important, however offhand it might seem. Even offhand is a thought-out thing.

But cool guys or not, good things were starting to happen to us. The very first time we went to Hawaii was in September 1968. This was a Dick Clark show in Honolulu, opening for Vanilla Fudge. We each got an airplane ticket and a hotel room—I think it was the Driftwood Hotel.

I get to my room, haven't been there but five minutes, and decide I'm going to go see Doug—maybe we can go for a walk. I go down to Doug's room. I'm knocking. No answer. I know we all just got to our room, so I knock again. Nothing.

"Hey, Cosmo, it's John."

I hear shuffling, some muffled voices.

"C'mon, Doug. Let's go to the beach. We gotta see Waikiki."

More shuffling. A mumbling voice. "No, I don't wanna go."

"Doug, what's goin' on?" He's not acting like my friend anymore.

I hear what sounds like another voice in there.

"Shit, Doug—you got *a girl* in there with you?"

I was shocked. We had not been in the hotel more than ten minutes. And what was going on in my psyche was, *Aw, are we gonna be like* that? *I didn't know we were gonna be like* those *bands. Really?*

Over the next few years, Doug certainly earned a reputation. Before anybody else had dropped their luggage on the floor, Doug had something going. He was the Rooster. And the whole world was his barnyard.

Now, I'm no saint, but at the time, I'm just a kid from El Cerrito, a little Boy Scout. And I'm feeling like, I'm amazingly disappointed. I guess you could say I'm not the guy who got into music to get girls—I was there for the music.

"Susie Q" was what I was into. Man, that song—the first piece of music we did that was in the major leagues. We'd finally stepped up out of the sandlots where the Golliwogs and the Blue Velvets were, and I knew it. *I knew* what to do. It was clear.

I was not afraid. I was superconfident, as a matter of fact. The only thing I was afraid of was the so-called sophomore jinx. The one-hit wonder. History is littered with the wreckage of all the one-hit wonders who failed on that second attempt. And I wanted to be the one that didn't. We had our one hit, and by God, I wasn't going back to the car wash. I didn't want to be a Golliwog again.

So I was ratcheting up the game and trying to inspire the people around me to do the same thing. With the guys in the band, I was able to talk a pretty good college rah-rah pep talk. I kept saying, "We have the spotlight! It's on *us!* And it'll stay there if we do something good. Otherwise, guess what?" When I looked at Fantasy Records and Saul Zaentz, I saw that they were clueless when it came to rock. We weren't on Columbia Records, that's for sure. I was on the smallest label in the whole world, and the advertising budget was fifteen cents. Saul wasn't going to spend any money—as Stu always said, "Saul's idea was, 'Spend pennies, make millions.'" We didn't have any machinery behind us, nor did we have anybody that understood that we needed that machinery. We didn't have a manager. We didn't have a publicist. So I took a hard look at all of this and said, "Well, I guess I'm just gonna have to do it with music."

The more music I do that's great, the more it'll overcome all those things that we don't have. I had to put on a work ethic like nobody ever saw before. I saw a musical career as something to work at. *Work.* I was really driven, and I'm proud of that. You might think that it's a curse or some kind of disease—it certainly isn't something you should keep on doing all your life, every day, forever. It's not healthy for yourself and those around you. But if you have a specific goal, a short-term goal, and you believe it's reachable, that's how you do it.

That meant I had to be a whirling dervish. My family and I were living on Kains Avenue in Albany, right outside El Cerrito. I had started to write songs for the next album, and I was putting a lot of thought into it. I had the luxury of a few months to write — time hadn't gotten compressed yet. We were living in a little apartment. In a lot of ways it was better than the house I had grown up in. It was new, and it had the cottage cheese ceiling, which I thought was cool then. At first we couldn't get a TV because I didn't have enough credit. I could barely write a check, with my twenty dollars a week from Tom and the little bit we'd gotten from our gigs.

There were no pictures or art on the wall — just a plain beige room. And I would sit on a little chair halfway between the "kitchen" and the front room, writing. I had my yellow pad of paper, and my little songwriting book. I would stay up every night into the wee hours, writing songs and arranging songs — it was literally all I thought about. For every good song there were twelve I rejected. I'd just sort of stare at the wall. I was slowed down, very much with my own thoughts. I discovered that I would kind of go into a trance, drinking coffee and smoking cigarettes. There were things that were not at hand, but in my mind, they could become very real to me. I was not stoned or drunk or anything like that, but as I concentrated, I would go deep.

I was trying to come up with something new. I was thinking, *Where's this thing going? What's it going to be?*

CHAPTER 8

I Guess I'm Just Gonna Have to Do It with Music

S ONGWRITING IS A tricky thing. You have to get real quiet, allow yourself to be alone. At least I do. Set aside time, or you'll never get to it. We're all very busy in our lives, and there's a lot of noise: the TV and your kids and their homework and your dog's barking, paying your bills, returning that crap you ordered because it doesn't fit—all the stuff of life. And songwriting is really much more in the opposite direction: it's about solitude and being quiet, because that's the only way that hidden stuff in your soul can finally be heard. You have to say to the world and to yourself, "I'm going to go to my room. I'm going to be quiet. I've got a guitar in my hand, a blank sheet of paper, and now here is the deal, right there."

Every writer will tell you: you sit down and face your blank sheet of paper. It is the most freeing thing in the world...and the most terrifying. You see, that blank page is a window to infinity. You can go anywhere, do anything, create something that has never existed before. It is curiosity and imagination, all mixed up with a lot of luck and pixie dust...while you pray for inspiration.